the unofficial
formula one history

the unofficial

formula one history

The illustrated story of a century of Grand Prix motor racing

mark hughes

foreword by **jenson button**

southwater

This edition is published by Southwater

Southwater is an imprint of Anness Publishing Ltd

Hermes House, 88–89 Blackfriars Road, London SE1 8HA

tel. 020 7401 2077; fax 020 7633 9499

www.southwaterbooks.com; info@anness.com

UK agent: The Manning Partnership Ltd, 6 The Old Dairy, Melcombe Road, Bath BA2 3LR
tel. 01225 478444; fax 01225 478440; sales@manning-partnership.co.uk

UK distributor: Grantham Book Services Ltd, Isaac Newton Way, Alma Park Industrial Estate,
Grantham, Lincs NG31 9SD; tel. 01476 541080; fax 01476 541061; orders@gbs.tbs-ltd.co.uk

North American agent/distributor: National Book Network, 4501 Forbes Boulevard, Suite 200,
Lanham, MD 20706; tel. 301 459 3366; fax 301 429 5746; www.nbnbooks.com

Australian agent/distributor: Pan Macmillan Australia, Level 18, St Martins Tower, 31 Market St,
Sydney, NSW 2000; tel. 1300 135 113; fax 1300 135 103; customer.service@macmillan.com.au

New Zealand agent/distributor: David Bateman Ltd, 30 Tarndale Grove, Off Bush Road,
Albany, Auckland; tel. (09) 415 7664; fax (09) 415 8892

A CIP catalogue record for this book is available from the British Library.

Publisher: Joanna Lorenz
Editor: Elizabeth Woodland
Production Controller: Darren Price
Senior Editor: Sarah Ainley
Text Editor: David Malsher
Design: Michael Morey
Photography: Sutton Motorsport Images

Previously published as part of a larger volume, *The Unofficial Complete
Encyclopedia of Formula One*

10 9 8 7 6 5 4 3 2 1

Contents

Foreword

"I've known Mark since I first came to Formula One in 2000. He's charted the various highs and lows of my career in the pages of *Autosport* with a lot of insight. Here he gives the full story of Grand Prix racing right from the very start up to the present day. There's technical stuff as well as sporting. It's a good read, and hopefully in some future edition it will tell the story of my first Grand Prix victory."

Jenson Button

▼ Jenson Button completed his first season with the BAR-Honda team in 2003 in superb form and led both the final races, in America and Japan.

▲ Jenson Button
at the 2003 German
Grand Prix.

▶ Jenson Button's
BAR-Honda at
Monaco in 2003.

Introduction

It was man's very nature that made motor racing so inevitable. Clever enough to have devised the car, he is intrinsically competitive enough to have then made racing cars a mere formality. The ultimate form of the discipline came to be called Grand Prix racing in 1906, just 11 years into the sport's history, and Formula One Grands Prix are still the pinnacle of the sport today. What also remains, unaltered through over a century, is the essence of the sport. The qualities it demands of drivers, who face the ultimate stakes, and technicians, who experience the most intense of challenges, make it arguably the most majestic of all sporting endeavours.

▼ David Coulthard winning in Australia in 2003.

▼ Kimi Raikkonen celebrates his first Grand Prix win in Malaysia in 2003.

Though latterly it has become more overtly commercial than in the past, that is simply a reflection of the world in which the sport exists, just as the cars have mirrored the level of technological sophistication of the modern industrial world. It shouldn't be forgotten that motorsport was conceived as much with business in mind – by a group of pioneer car manufacturers – as it was for sport. Formula One owes its existence to business, and always has, but the superficial trappings melt away to nothing in the intensity of battle, once the start flag has dropped or the lights have gone out. Between that moment and the chequered flag, the sport exists in its purest form.

▼ The youngest winner: Fernando Alonso at the Hungarian Grand Prix in 2003.

▼ Michael Schumacher takes championship number six.

The History of Formula One

The thread of the sport's lineage is long and sometimes complex. But it is very clearly a thread, a brilliantly vivid one in which heroes have been made, celebrated and – over the decades – largely forgotten. The nature of the sport gives it a here and now intensity, and leaves the past in black and white dusty memory. But revisiting the deeds of the drivers, the manufacturers, engineers and designers can bring their achievements back to life, and lend them their true perspective. Here, we look at the men, the cars and the races that made their mark on history, stretching from the first true motor race in 1895 right up to the present day.

◀ Ayrton Senna's last race. Senna's Williams FW16 follows the safety car at Imola, 1 May 1994.

The Seeds are Sown

Motor racing is very nearly as old as the motor car itself. Karl Benz and Gottlieb Daimler are widely credited with the invention of the car – each had their first petrol-fired prototypes running in 1885 – and within a decade the first significant motor race took place.

In the early years cars did not race round and round, but from place to place. The organizers did not charge an admission fee to watch, and the cars were not recognizably different from those driven as a means of transport. But the sport's essence, to get from the start to the finish against both the clock and each other, was exactly as it has been ever since.

The First Race

Although the car was born in Germany, France can be said to have invented motorsport. The first true race was a contest from Paris to Bordeaux and back, a distance of just over 1190 kilometres (740 miles) on public highways. Twenty-seven vehicles congregated at Porte Maillot in the early hours of 11 June 1895 and, one by one, were sent on their way. Only those in the car – of whom there had to be at least two – were allowed to work on the car during the race, using only those tools carried with them.

The event was devised by a group of pioneer manufacturers with the

▲ Emile Levassor's Panhard-Levassor car in the 1894 Paris–Rouen reliability trial that led to the 1895 race.

idea of publicizing the practicality and speed of the motor car. The winner, Emile Levassor, was a partner in the firm of Panhard et Levassor, an old French engineering company that had recently embraced car manufacture. Levassor's drive was heroic. He had

planned to change over with his relief driver some time before Bordeaux but, finding him asleep at around 3am, decided to continue. In fact, he drove the entire event, and the relief driver became simply a passenger. As he passed each time control still in command of the race, news of Levassor's epic solo performance spread like wildfire and when he arrived back in Paris in the afternoon of 13 June,

▲ Chevalier René de Knyff seated on the Panhard-Levassor car that won the first Paris–Bordeaux race in 1898.

◄ Degrais competing in the Paris–Madrid race of 1903.

▼ Callan is pictured here in his Wolseley motor during the Circuit des Ardennes race, Belgium, 1903.

thousands were there to greet him. With an average speed of just under 24km/h (15mph), he was five hours ahead of the next man. The new sport had its first hero.

The heat of competition fed a technology drive that advanced the car at breakneck speed – to the great benefit of the customers. Pneumatic tyres and the steering wheel were just two of the more obvious advances the sport generated in its early years. By 1901, racing machines were capable of up to 120km/h (80mph). Meanwhile, sales of the motor car soared: France produced 13,000 of them in 1903.

The First Tragedy

The sport's honeymoon period came to an abrupt end later that same year. Millions of spectators lined the route of the Paris–Madrid race in May 1903 to watch in awe the cars that were, by now, powered by monstrous engines of up to 14 litres. It was a tragedy waiting to unfold. Competitors Marcel Renault, Lorraine Barrow, Philip Stead

and two riding mechanics were all killed in various brutal accidents along the route. But the biggest, most unacceptable tragedy occurred in the town of Chatellerault, when a child walked into the road and a soldier ran to pull him clear. Tourand's car hit them, killing both, before veering into the crowd, killing one spectator and injuring many more.

As cars and distraught competitors rested overnight in Bordeaux, the French government stepped in and stopped the race. The silent cars were pulled to a train by horse and transported back to Paris. City-to-city racing was over.

▼ Fernand Gabriel wins the 1903 Paris–Bordeaux race in a Mors that produced 70hp. It marked the end of city-to-city racing.

From Cities to Circuits

The tragedy of the 1903 Paris–Madrid race came close to killing the sport for ever. It was only granted a reprieve by a saner approach. No longer would races run through major towns with big population centres; they would instead utilize the roads of sparsely populated rural areas. More critically, no longer would the races run from place to place, but instead around roads comprising circuits, thus making the routes easier to police.

The New Era of Circuit Racing

The first major event of the new format had been the 1902 Circuit des Ardennes in Belgium, ironically the race that immediately preceded the 1903 Paris–Madrid. The race comprised six laps of an 80-kilometre (50-mile) circuit of public roads through the countryside, and was won by Englishman Charles Jarrott in his French Panhard.

The success of the event and the end of city-to-city racing meant that the Circuit des Ardennes became the blueprint for the new era of the sport. One of the first post-tragedy races run to this new format was the Gordon

Bennett Cup, held in pre-republic Ireland in 1903.

Gordon Bennett was a millionaire newspaper magnate and a vital early supporter of motor racing. As well as helping to fund the first races and

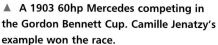

▲ A 1903 60hp Mercedes competing in the Gordon Bennett Cup. Camille Jenatzy's example won the race.

giving them the lifeblood of publicity through one of his publications, the *Paris Herald*, he also devised the competition that made the sport truly international, and that bore his name.

The Gordon Bennett series was first held in 1900. Countries could enter up to three cars each in the race. From 1903 each country was identified by the colours of its cars. The winning nation would host the following year's event. France dominated initially but, in winning the 1902 event for Britain (by virtue of being the only finisher), Selwyn Francis Edge ensured that the Royal Automobile Club had to have an Act of Parliament passed to host the 1903 race in Ireland; racing on the public highway had always been forbidden by British law.

Camille Jenatzy won the race for Mercedes, and thereby took the event to Germany for 1904. The French industry didn't take kindly to being beaten in

◀ Christian Lautenschlager was first to the finish in a Mercedes in the 1908 French Grand Prix at Dieppe.

what it saw as its own specialist field, and after winning the event in 1904 and being the winning host in 1905, the French declined to stage the event the following year. The Automobile Club de France had instead devised another competition in which no restrictions would be put on the number of entrants a country could provide. The name of this competition was the "Grand Prix". Its lineage continues to this day.

The First Grand Prix

Held at Le Mans in 1906, the inaugural Grand Prix was won by the Renault of Ferenc Szisz, a Hungarian who had previously been Louis Renault's riding mechanic in the city-to-city races. The event was a great success and other countries copied its format, though it would be many years before the term "Grand Prix" was applied to races outside of France. For now, the USA came the closest, with its American "Grand Prize".

For the 1908 event, the Paris-based international governing body of the sport formulated regulations to ensure uniformity from country to country. Motor racing flourished, even surviving a mass pull-out by manufacturers concerned at spiralling costs and the first downturn of sales. As early pioneers such as Panhard and Mors faded, Mercedes remained very much

a central force and was joined by Fiat and Peugeot.

By 1914, on the eve of World War I, the French Grand Prix attracted 13 manufacturers and 33 cars. The race saw an epic fight between the twin-cam 16-valve Peugeot of Georges Boillot and the might of the Mercedes team. Christian Lautenschlager's Mercedes won after Boillot retired on the last lap. The engine of Lautenschlager's car was based on that which would soon be put to use in fighter planes.

▲ Vincenzo Lancia in his Fiat at the very first Grand Prix, held near Le Mans, France, in 1906.

▼ *(left)* The front cover of the French periodical *La Vie au Grand Air* shows Hungarian driver Ferenc Szisz at the wheel. He was the winner of the first recognized Grand Prix held near Le Mans in 1906.

▼ *(right)* Ferenc Szisz in his Renault at Le Mans, 1906. Szisz and the French manufacturer won the race that year.

Boom Between Wars

The armistice period that followed World War I accelerated the pace of technology, and lessons learned there were soon applied in motorsport. Advances made in metallurgy and in understanding the combustion process more fully meant that engine efficiency rocketed. The 1921 Fiat's 8-cylinder motor became the blueprint for racing engines for decades to come.

Grand Prix Racing Spreads

In 1922, the new Monza track near Milan hosted the Italian Grand Prix. This was a purpose-built race circuit – it was the first time a major European race hadn't been held on public roads – and it enabled Grand Prix race promoters to charge spectators an entrance fee for the first time. Soon afterwards, other tracks were built in a similar vein, such as Montlhéry on the outskirts of Paris, and Sitges just south of Barcelona.

Most of the races continued to be run on public roads however, and in order to stop speeds escalating out of control, a 2-litre formula was imposed for 1922. This signalled a parting of the ways between European and American

▲ Rudolf Caracciola in his Mercedes-Benz on his way to winning the 1937 Swiss Grand Prix. German cars now dominated racing.

▼ Luigi Fagioli (Mercedes) passing Soffietti (Maserati) at the 1935 Monaco Grand Prix.

▼ Independent team owners came to the fore from the mid-1920s to early 1930s.

racing which, until this time, had overlapped. The American Duesenberg team had won the 1921 French Grand Prix, while European cars had dominated for a time at the Indianapolis 500. American racing was chiefly conducted on closed tracks, not public roads, and with its wide open spaces, the American car industry was producing passenger cars with ever-bigger engines: the new European 2-litre formula was an irrelevance there.

The Pioneering Teams

Such was Fiat's dominance during the early 1920s that rival manufacturers had to resort to poaching technical staff from Fiat in order to compete. It was in this way that Alfa Romeo and Sunbeam became serious Grand Prix forces, with the former team being advised by one of its drivers, Enzo Ferrari. Sunbeam became the first British constructor to win a Grand Prix, when Henry Segrave triumphed in France in 1923.

The economic downturn of the late 1920s saw manufacturers pull out of the sport and, for a time, wealthy independent team owners formed its backbone, with specialist car companies such as Bugatti and Maserati providing the hardware. It was during this time that Tazio Nuvolari graduated to the sport from motorcycle racing, and created such a sensation that he is still often cited as the greatest driver who ever lived.

Hitler came to power in Germany early in 1933, and he immediately identified Grand Prix racing as a powerful tool in propagating the image of Aryan superiority. Backed by Nazi subsidies, Mercedes-Benz and Auto Union entered the competition with revolutionary new models in 1934 that rendered the various Italian and French machinery completely obsolete. Their independent suspensions allowed huge horsepower gains to be utilized and, before long, speeds of up to 320km/h (200mph) were being reached. The German domination continued until the cessation of Grand Prix racing on 1 September 1939, the day that Britain declared war on Nazi Germany.

◄ *(left to right)* Manfred von Brauchitsch, Christian Kautz, Tazio Nuvolari and Hermann Muller at the Donington Grand Prix, Donington Park, England, in 1938.

▼ Tazio Nuvolari, Auto Union, during the 1938 Italian Grand Prix.

Post-war Recovery

During the period of German domination before the outbreak of World War II, several constructors had turned instead to voiturette (small car) racing. With Germany in no position to partake in international motorsport in the early post-war years, pre-war voiturette Alfa Romeos, Maseratis and ERAs formed the basis of an early revival of the sport.

The Birth of Formula One

The reconstituted governing body arranged a loose calendar of "premier" Grands Prix for 1947, and for the following year it announced a new Grand Prix formula: Formula One. Sensibly, it catered for existing machinery and was therefore largely based on the pre-war voiturette formula, which allowed for supercharged engines of 1.5 litres. As a means of bolstering the grids, Formula One also catered for unsupercharged engines of up to 4.5 litres, in order to encourage the entry of the sportscar-derived racers that had performed a similar makeweight class in the immediate pre-war period.

With their Italian factories in ruins, wheeling out their pre-war cars and winning some Grands Prix was a vital tonic for Alfa Romeo, which was the dominant racing force in these early post-war years. Ironically the car – dubbed the "Alfetta" – had been created under the guidance of Enzo Ferrari, who had now ceased to be Alfa's racing manager and had instead

▲ Froilán González wins his own and Ferrari's first Championship-status Grand Prix at Silverstone in 1951, defeating the previously all-conquering Alfa Romeos.

become a constructor in his own right. Alfa's financial plight precluded it from taking part during 1949 and, in their absence, the Ferrari marque racked up its first Grand Prix victories.

▲ The Argentinian Juan Manuel Fangio, five times World Champion.

◄ Juan Manuel Fangio in his Alfa Romeo 158 during the 1950 International Trophy at Silverstone.

▼ Juan Manuel Fangio in his Alfa Romeo 158 Alfetta during the Belgian Grand Prix, at Spa-Francorchamps in 1950.

▲ Giuseppe Farina pictured at home, shortly after winning the first Drivers' World Championship in 1950. He won the British, Swiss and Italian Grands Prix.

The World Championships

Alfa was tempted into a return in 1950 by the inauguration of a World Championship. In a move designed to regain the sport its pre-war following by popularizing its appeal, the contest would find a "World Champion" driver Points were awarded based on the results of six nominated Grands Prix. The first race of the World Championship was held round the perimeter track of a disused British wartime airfield called Silverstone. Actually, all of the Grands Prix were held on European soil, but the "world" title was justified by the inclusion of results from the American Indianapolis 500 race. This anomaly continued for much of the decade until genuine Grands Prix outside Europe began to appear on the calendar.

Alfa Romeo won every Grand Prix in 1950, and the title contest was fought out between their drivers Giuseppe Farina and Juan Manuel Fangio. The former just got the verdict on account of a better reliability record, though it was the Argentinian Fangio who set the pace. Fangio went on to his first world title in 1951, but from mid-season of that year, his supercharged Alfa Romeo was pushed hard by a new challenger – the unsupercharged V12 Ferrari.

Technology 1951

Ferrari 375

After trying – but failing – to beat Alfa Romeo with a similar 1.5-litre supercharged car in 1950, Enzo Ferrari and his designer Aurelio Lampredi re-assessed. They had noted that the pre-war 4.5-litre unsupercharged Talbots could occasionally push the much more powerful Alfas uncomfortably close over a race distance by virtue of using less fuel and therefore making fewer refuelling stops. The rationale behind the 375 of 1951 was of a 4.5-litre car more modern than the Talbots that would retain an economy advantage over the Alfas but close the power deficit. Its V12 engine produced around 330bhp at a time when the Alfas were giving over 400bhp, but critically it consumed fuel at around 7.2km/g (4.5mpg) rather than the 2.9km/g (1.8mpg) of its rival, which had such high supercharger boost pressure that fuel was needed for cooling as well as combustion. The turning point came at Silverstone in 1951, when José Froilán González was able to run his 375 wheel-to-wheel with Fangio's Alfa, and then pull clear when the supercharged car had to make its inevitable early pit stop. Enzo Ferrari was famously quoted as saying he felt as if he had killed his mother, given his former close links with Alfa.

▼ José Froilán González on his way to the first Championship-status Grand Prix win for Ferrari at Silverstone in 1951.

Ferrari Maintain Italy's Lead

Ferrari's speed in the second half of 1951 put Alfa Romeo on the defensive. As the newer design was honed into an ever-faster machine, the development potential of the Alfetta – which had debuted in 1937 – hit a brick wall. Having retained the championship by the skin of their teeth, and without the finances to design and build a new model, Alfa made an honourable withdrawal at the end of the year.

Switch to Formula Two

The departure of Alfa Romeo left Formula One with a problem: Ferrari now had no worthwhile competition. Maserati was operating on a hand-to-mouth basis, building and selling outclassed cars while making plans for the future. There was the almost mythical BRM, an exciting idea borne of British post-war optimism and

▼ **Belgian Grand Prix 1952: Alberto Ascari in his Ferrari. The Italian won every Grand Prix he contested for a dominant season.**

▲ **Ascari in the Ferrari 375 at the 1951 German Grand Prix. This marked his first Championship-status victory.**

Shapers

Enzo Ferrari

The founder of the most revered of all racing teams described the essence of his ability as "a flair for the agitation of men". Ruthless and autocratic, he was also shrewd and single-minded, traits that were evident from his days as racing manager for Alfa Romeo in the 1920s, right up to his death in 1988. He was a moderately successful driver in the early 1920s, but his real value to Alfa came as an organizer; it was he who succeeded in poaching key technical staff from Fiat, for instance. His links with Alfa were finally severed in the late 1930s, and in 1948 the first Grand Prix car bearing the name of "Ferrari" appeared on the track.

His relationships with his drivers and other key personnel were often stormy as the success of his race team overrode any human considerations, though for certain rare men – Peter Collins in the 1950s and Gilles Villeneuve in the 1980s being the most notable – he made exceptions.

financed by that country's industry. The power potential of its supercharged V16 engine was said to be fantastic, but no-one knew for sure because it never hung together long enough to find out. It was a frail hope on which to rest a World Championship contest.

Race promoters, fearing no-one would come to watch a Ferrari demonstration, switched their main races to Formula Two, a junior category for 2-litre unsupercharged cars. The governing body followed suit and announced that the 1952 and 1953 World Championships would be for Formula Two cars. Ironically, Ferrari dominated anyway, with its lead driver Alberto Ascari achieving a sequence of successes that has yet to be equalled. He won six of the seven Grands Prix comprising the 1952 season, followed by a further five in 1953, and in the course of his run he established a record of nine consecutive victories that still stands today.

Ascari's luck ran out in the final race of 1953, at Monza, where he lost a thrilling battle to chief rival Fangio, who was driving the ever-improving Formula Two Maserati. Ascari and Fangio, the two fastest drivers in the world at the time, shared the front row of the grid, but the latter made a poor start as Ascari surged into the lead ahead of his Ferrari team-mate, Farina. Fangio's friend and Maserati team-mate Onofré Marimon then slipstreamed past both Ferraris to lead as Fangio made up the lost ground and made it a four-car slipstreaming battle. Time after time, the positions changed between the four until, at half-distance, Marimon was forced to pit with a radiator leak. He rejoined a lap down but, crucially, still with the leaders on the road.

Into the last corner of the last lap, Farina made a desperate bid for victory, and leader Ascari spun trying to avoid contact as Farina ran wide. The spinning Ascari was hit by Marimon, allowing Fangio to nip through for his first victory since breaking his neck at this same track the year before.

▶ **Alberto Ascari and Ferrari took their second World Championship title in 1953.**

▲ **Ascari leads Fangio, Farina and Marimon in the battle of the 1953 Italian Grand Prix.**

◀ **Ascari takes the plaudits again in 1953. His sequence of nine consecutive wins is a record that has not yet been broken.**

The Brief Return of the Factories

Motor racing had been invented by the big European customer-car producers, and largely dominated by them until the advent of World War II. Thereafter, with their factories in ruins, they had little choice but to stay out of it, Alfa Romeo's flurry with their pre-war cars notwithstanding.

The Specialists

In their place, the sport came to be dominated by specialist race car constructors, such as Ferrari, Maserati and Gordini, who built cars for sale to race entrants and ran their own teams of "works" machines. The specialist constructors existed on revenue from the sale of their machines, from start and finish money from race organizers, and from trade deals with suppliers who could then advertise their part in the ensuing success.

But in 1954, with the post-war recovery process now well established, the factories began to return. First Mercedes-Benz, then Lancia announced Grand Prix programmes and the fact that they had respectively signed Fangio and Ascari, the top two Grand Prix drivers, signalled the seriousness of their intent.

▲ Lancia's D50 was an even more advanced design than the rival Mercedes.

The Return to Formula One

With such an undertaking of support, the governing body felt confident in the reintroduction of Formula One as the basis for the World Championship. This time the formula stipulated engines of no more than 2.5 litres unsupercharged. Ferrari and Maserati came up with new

▼ Mercedes-Benz W196 *Stromlinienwagen* exiting Champel Curve at Silverstone in 1954. The streamlined body of the car did not suit the airfield circuit.

machines, but when Mercedes unveiled the W196 racer, the different scale of their resources became very clear.

Fangio gave the car a win first time out, in the 1954 French Grand Prix, with his team-mate Karl Kling close behind, and the rest nowhere. For the remainder of the season, the Mercedes would be beaten only twice, and Fangio duly delivered the Championship – something he repeated for the company after an even more dominant performance in 1955, this time backed up by the highly promising young British driver, Stirling Moss, who took his first victory that year at Aintree.

▼ Stirling Moss in his Maserati 250F at the 1954 British Grand Prix. He retired from second place with only ten laps to go.

The Factories Withdraw Again

The introduction of the Lancia D50 had been delayed until the end of 1954, but it set pole position by a full second in its debut race, and looked set to give Ascari victory before breaking down. In concept it was arguably even more advanced than the Mercedes, but the financial problems of the parent company meant its potential was ultimately untapped. Ascari's death while testing a Ferrari sports racer in May gave Lancia the justification it needed to withdraw from the sport at the end of 1955.

Mercedes withdrew too, for reasons even more catastrophic. In by far the biggest tragedy the sport has ever suffered, over 80 spectators were killed in the 1955 Le Mans 24 Hours sportscar race, when a Mercedes was launched into the crowd after hitting another car. The fall-out affected all of motor racing and several Grands Prix were immediately cancelled. Mercedes suddenly found its participation in the sport changed from a public relations benefit to a liability, and it pulled out at the end of that year, not to return for a very, very long time. All of which, of course, left Formula One back in the hands of the specialists, with significant long-term consequences.

Technology 1955

Mercedes W196

Innovation and attention to detail was everywhere on this landmark racer. Its eight cylinders were fed by inlet and outlet valves that were not closed by conventional springs but by "desmodronic" actuation, whereby they were directly mechanically controlled for more accuracy and reliability. Its chassis was not the conventional metal ladder frame with bolstering tubing. Instead, the tubing was arranged in such a way that its geometry formed a load-bearing structure and the heavy ladder frame was dispensed with; this was termed "spaceframe" construction. Its brake drums were initially mounted inboard

▲ The two Mercedes-Benz W196, driven by Juan Mauel Fangio and Karl Kling, receive attention behind the pits. Fangio has his back to the camera, on the left.

rather than within the wheels, thus reducing the unsprung mass of the car, to the benefit of road-holding. But the most visually dramatic feature was its all-enveloping bodywork that made traditional open-wheelers look previous-generation. Ironically, this induced a handling imbalance and the car more usually ran in more conventional open-wheel form.

▼ The enclosed-wheel "streamliner" bodywork was only used occasionally.

The Unstoppable Fangio

▼ Five times Formula One World title holder Juan Manuel Fangio driving through Becketts in the Ferrari D50.

The specialist constructors were quick to take advantage of the factory withdrawals. Enzo Ferrari's shrewdness was never more apparent than when he contrived to get paid for taking over the assets of the Lancia Grand Prix project – including the D50 cars, which were a big advance over the existing Ferraris. Fangio was signed up to drive them and he duly delivered the 1956 Championship, his fourth and Ferrari's third.

Fangio and Ferrari

But it was a far from smooth road to glory for both parties. Enzo Ferrari and Fangio failed to hit it off, and there was a lot of tension and mutual distrust in the team. As they arrived at Monza for the final round of the title contest, Fangio's biggest threat was his own team-mate, Peter Collins, the young British driver, who was a particular favourite of the boss.

Fangio was in the leading group, a couple of places ahead of Collins, when he suffered a steering-arm breakage on lap 18 and pulled into the pits to retire the car. At that time, teams were allowed to use more than one driver in a single car and have them share the points. When the third Ferrari driver, Luigi Musso, pitted to refuel, he was asked if he would hand his car over to Fangio. He refused.

This meant that Collins, now in third place, stood poised to win the title. But when he came in for a tyre stop on the 35th lap and saw Fangio standing watching, he immediately jumped out and offered his car to him. Fangio took it and with it finished second – enough to clinch him the title. It was a supreme act of sportsmanship from Collins. Asked why he had done it, he simply replied, "Because Fangio deserved it." Fangio was indebted.

▲ Fangio (2) behind the lead car, in action for Maserati.

◄ Juan Manuel Fangio takes the winner's garland after winning the 1956 German Grand Prix.

Maserati and "That" Race

Fangio was approaching 47 years old as the 1957 season began. He had originally planned to retire at the end of 1955, but an economic crisis in his home country of Argentina had persuaded him to continue. But any thoughts that his competitive spirit was waning were utterly demolished in 1957. Neither he nor Ferrari had any interest in continuing their partnership, and he switched instead to Maserati, who had continually refined and developed their 250F model over the last three years until it was a beautifully responsive and balanced machine, just the sort of car in which Fangio could display his genius.

At the German Grand Prix, Fangio clinched that year's Championship – his fifth – with his final Grand Prix victory. It was also his greatest. Around the mountainous 14-mile Nürburgring

◄ Juan Manuel Fangio in his Maserati at Monza in 1957.

▼ Mike Hawthorn and Peter Collins lead Fangio's Maserati at the German Grand Prix of 1957.

circuit, he overcame a mid-race delay in the pits to claw back a 51-second deficit, a task that had looked impossible. He broke and re-broke the lap record on each subsequent lap, leaving it at 9 minutes 17.4 seconds, over 8 seconds faster than his own pole position time. The Ferrari drivers were unable to respond, and he passed them both on the last lap. Fangio later recalled that on that day he had driven at a level he had never reached before, and did not wish to reach again. Many regard it as the greatest race ever driven.

The British Challenge

Britain had enjoyed its moments of Grand Prix glory, but never for any great duration. Sunbeam had won races in the 1920s in partnership with Henry Segrave before becoming financially strapped. In the late 1930s, rising British star Richard Seaman displayed such immense promise that he was employed by the Nazi-backed Mercedes team and actually won the 1938 German Grand Prix. He suffered a fatal accident while leading the 1939 Belgian Grand Prix.

The New British Breed

What occurred in the 1950s was quite different; it was a movement, and for the first time it became conceivable that the centre of motor racing might move away from France and Italy, its twin homes for half a century.

British law had never allowed the road racing seen in those countries, and consequently British motorsport initially took a different direction, being centred around the specially-built enclosed circuit of Brooklands. This was in

essence an oval shape: no corners, just flat-out running around a dramatic, banked track. The demands of this sort of racing were rather different to those of traditional road circuit-based Grands Prix. But World War II rendered Brooklands unusable as a race track as

▲ **Tony Brooks** (left) **and Stirling Moss after winning the 1957 British Grand Prix. Moss took over Brooks' car after his own suffered problems.**

▼ **Harry Schell drives his Vanwall at Castle Combe in 1955.**

much of it was demolished to make room for expanded aircraft-manufacturing facilities.

What the war gave British motor racing in place of Brooklands were dozens of redundant wartime airfields. These made ideal race venues, and the tracks more nearly reproduced the demands of continental road racing. Concurrent with this, the country's governing body, the RAC, approved a new low-cost, entry-level class of racing, Formula 500 (later renamed Formula Three). This catered for motorcycle-engined cars of 500cc and attracted an entirely new breed of driver to British sport. No longer was it exclusively an idle pastime of wealthy men; it attracted ambitious young

talent who wished to become professionals. Stirling Moss and Peter Collins were the outstanding graduate drivers of this formula. Among their rivals were three men later to have a huge influence on Grand Prix racing outside of the cars: John Cooper, Ken Tyrrell and Bernie Ecclestone. The 750 Motor Club, another post-war British attempt at low-cost motorsport, was meanwhile proving incredibly fertile ground for engineering talent, with Colin Chapman as its vanguard.

Vandervell and British Success

Concurrent with these movements was another British initiative, but a private one: that of the industrialist Tony Vandervell. He had become a very wealthy man as the boss of Vandervell Bearings, whose patented "thinwall bearing" was behind major efficiency gains in aircraft and car engines. With the aim of one day having his own

Grand Prix team, he initially bought customer Formula One race cars from Enzo Ferrari. Called the "Thinwall Specials", these modified Ferraris were the precursors to the Vanwall, which first appeared in 1955. Using his industry contacts to the full, Vandervell

commissioned de Havilland aircraft aerodynamicist Frank Costin to design a highly advanced body, while the engine was a scaled-up version of that used in Norton motorcycle racers. By 1957, it was the fastest car in Formula One, and Stirling Moss and Tony Brooks took it to a shared victory in the British Grand Prix of that year. It was the first wave of British success, and was soon to be followed up in devastating fashion as the young racing community that had built up around Formula 500 transformed itself from a movement to a revolution. In the space of a couple of seasons, the whole fabric of Formula One had changed fundamentally.

▲ *(left)* British driver Stirling Moss in his Vanwall at Aintree for the 1957 British and European Grand Prix, where he lapped at 144.5km/h (89.85mph).

◄ The young Stirling Moss with his 500cc Formula Three car.

Walls Come Tumbling Down

"Suddenly, there were green cars all around me. I wasn't part of that world. I drove red cars. It was time to leave." The words are those of Juan Manuel Fangio, who retired part-way through the 1958 season after a record five world titles, four of them in the Italian colours of red. British racing green had reached a landmark in the 1957 Italian Grand Prix, where the race organizers had to change the grid formation to 4-3-4 from the usual 3-2-3, in order to get an Italian car onto the front row. The fastest three qualifiers were Vanwalls.

British Racing Green

For 1958, a new world title was initiated – for constructors. This ran alongside the Drivers' Championship. Vanwall won it, but their success was spread between Moss and Brooks, who were therefore pipped to the Drivers' Championship by Ferrari's Mike Hawthorn (and even he was British). Ferrari effectively had only one driver in the championship fight after the

▲ **A relaxed Mike Hawthorn in the pits during practice for the British Grand Prix at Silverstone in 1956. Driving the BRM P25, Hawthorn was an early leader in the race, but he soon retired.**

death in the German Grand Prix of Peter Collins.

But for all the glory days enjoyed by the streamlined, thoroughbred Vanwalls, the year's most significant victory went to a tiny, runtish-looking jumped-up Formula Two car, also British. Called a Cooper, it won the opening race of the season in Argentina. Driven in this race by Moss, it signalled the arrival into the rarefied Grand Prix ranks of the Formula 500 movement.

Because the cars of Formula 500 had used motorcycle engines with chain-drives, the logical place to put the engine had been between the driver and the driven rear wheels. This brought further, unforeseen, advantages. The pre-war Auto Unions had been "mid-engined" too, but they were monster cars whose size disguised the superiority of the layout, and thus left it unexploited until the Coopers – father and son, Charles and John – came along.

The Coopers Pave the Way

Because Formula One had been the preserve of small specialist teams since the pull-out of Mercedes and Lancia, the engineering was not progressive. As specialists rooted in the fabric of Grand Prix racing, Ferrari and Maserati had neither the resources nor the breadth of vision to fundamentally re-evaluate; they simply honed and refined. Vanwall, another specialist, had been created in the image of Ferrari. But Cooper came from leftfield, from different roots entirely, and they were not constrained by any convention other than those established in a very young junior formula.

It soon became clear that the funny little car with its engine in the "wrong" place – which had precipitated jeers of derision when it first turned up at practice in Argentina 1958 – had made instant dinosaurs of thoroughbreds. The DNA of the Grand Prix car had just been altered.

◄ **Mike Hawthorn laps Giulio Cabianca on the start/finish straight of Monza in 1958. Hawthorn finished second.**

▲ The supremely gifted Stirling Moss, who, along with Tony Brooks, helped British Formula One racing take on the Italians.

▲ Moss winning the 1957 Pescara Grand Prix in his Vanwall, one of the three victories they took that year.

▼ Tony Brooks, for Vanwall, wins the Belgian Grand Prix at the Spa-Francorchamps circuit in 1958.

Front Engine's Last Goodbyes

There was to be no stopping Cooper in 1959. The car with which Moss had won the Argentinian Grand Prix in 1958 had not been a proper Grand Prix machine, merely a Formula Two car with a slightly enlarged engine.

The "Garagistes"
Encouraged by this success, the Coopers set about building a proper Formula One car. But though its lines were sleeker, and its engine more powerful, it was built very much to the formula of their breakthrough Argentina car. Not only did it retain the mid-engined layout, but it utilized parts from wherever they could be found, and adapted them as required: a gearbox based on that of a road-going Citroën, key suspension parts borrowed from the Volkswagen Beetle, and steering components from a Triumph. The engine was bought in from Coventry Climax, who had developed it out of what was originally a fire-pump motor.

If Ferrari and Maserati, who always made their own engines and components, had been previously considered racing "specialists" to distinguish them from the big

▲ **Tony Brooks won the 1959 French Grand Prix in his Ferrari Dino 246 V6, but by then he was fighting against the tide of Coopers.**

car-producing factories, this took the concept several stages further. Cooper simply designed and assembled their cars and used a network of specialized sub-contractors to provide necessary hardware. Enzo Ferrari contemptuously described them as "garagistes". He also famously said his cars would never have mid-mounted engines as "the horse should pull the cart, not push it".

Here to Stay
The network of racing specialists that had formed in Britain around Cooper and the Formula 500 movement was soon servicing other constructors.

▼ **Jack Brabham's Cooper on the Oporto circuit of the Portuguese Grand Prix in 1960.**

Technology 1959

Cooper T51

A centralization of the car's masses was the critical advantage endowed by the mid-engined layout. In much the same way that a door with heavy weights bolted to the middle would be easier to move than one with the weights bolted to the outer edge, the mid-engined car was able to change direction quicker and with less momentum. In scientific terms, it had a lower "polar moment of inertia" than a traditional front-engined car.

The benefits of the layout multiplied. Because the front of the car didn't have to accommodate the engine, it could have a lower frontal area, making it quicker down the straight and more economical. Because no propshaft was needed to carry drive from a front engine to rear wheels, the car could be lower, giving benefits on the straights and in the corners. No propshaft and a lower

body meant it could be smaller and lighter, and therefore quicker to accelerate, brake and manoeuvre. The 1959 Cooper weighed in at 460kg, a massive 20 per cent lighter than the rival Ferrari 246. Even with 60 brake horsepower less, the Cooper had it covered. The weight and aerodynamic benefits meant less fuel was needed,

▲ Masten Gregory driving a Formula One Cooper T51 at Aintree in 1959.

furthering its weight advantage at the start. The lower weight also made it gentler on its tyres, which would thereby retain their grip for longer. The advantages for car and driver just kept snowballing.

A whole community of geographically close teams formed in the south of England, knowledge between them spread fast, and soon these "garagistes" were dominating the Grand Prix grids.

That community has formed the mainstay of Formula One ever since.

Ferrari's beautiful front-engined dinosaurs fought valiantly against an irresistible tide in 1959, and their driver

Tony Brooks was unlucky to miss out on the championship to Cooper's Jack Brabham. But there was no going back. Formula One had changed for ever and mid-engined cars were here to stay.

▲ Jack Brabham, driving for Cooper, was the 1959 World Champion.

▶ Tony Brooks' front-engined Ferrari (24) fights it out with Jack Brabham's rear-engined Cooper (8) in the 1959 French Grand Prix.

Rear-engine Revolution Completed

With a further development of their mid-engined wondercar, Cooper steamrollered their way to the 1960 World Championship – again with Jack Brabham as their driver – in a yet more convincing demonstration of the layout's superiority.

Ferrari Converts

As Ferrari continued to campaign hopelessly outdated front-engined machines, they were left outclassed, and even Enzo Ferrari was forced to eat his words about the horse pushing the cart. At the Monaco Grand Prix, his team debuted a prototype that had been crudely converted to the mid-engined layout. The lessons learned from this were applied as the team effectively wrote off the 1960 season to prepare for 1961, when a new 1.5-litre (unsupercharged) formula was due to replace the 2.5-litre one that had run since 1954.

Cooper and Lotus

The closest rival to Cooper in 1960 was another British constructor, Lotus. Using the same bought-in Coventry Climax engines as Cooper, and relying on the same network of specialist

sub-contractors, Lotus built their first mid-engined car for the 1960 season. Team boss Colin Chapman had a reputation as a brilliantly original thinker from his days in the 750 Motor Club in Britain. It was partly his pride in this reputation that had prevented him

▼ Jack Brabham, winner of the Portuguese Grand Prix, 1960, in the Cooper T53. Brabham benefited from the absence for much of that season of Stirling Moss.

▲ Jack Brabham, winner of the British Grand Prix, 1960, in the Cooper T53, on his way to a second successive world title. This confirmed front-engined cars were dead.

from copying the Cooper mid-engined formula earlier; Lotus had struggled with front-engined Formula One cars in 1958 and 1959.

With his Lotus 18, Chapman combined the Cooper's layout with a much more scientific approach.

▲ After giving Cooper its first Grand Prix victory in Argentina in 1958, Moss continued to rack up wins for the marque in 1959.

The spaceframe chassis had a more sophisticated geometry, and the suspension was designed to give the tyres an easier time. His obsession with weight reduction was reflected in a kerb weight of just 390kg, still the lightest winning Grand Prix car of all time. As part of the 1961 regulations, the sport's governing body stipulated a minimum weight of 450kg, fearing that cars such as the Lotus were frail. Regulation minimum weights have been a feature of Formula One ever since.

Maybe the fear was justified. Stirling Moss gave the Lotus its first victory at Monaco in 1960, but two races later broke his back when practising for the Belgian Grand Prix. He was thrown out of the car after crashing because a rear wheel had fallen off due to hub failure. It put Moss out for most of the year, and gave Brabham and Cooper their relatively easy runs to the Drivers' and Constructors' Championships.

▼ **Winner Jack Brabham in the Cooper T53 at the British Grand Prix, Silverstone, 1960.**

Shapers

John Cooper

John Cooper and his father Charles founded Cooper Cars in the late 1940s to produce machines for the new British Formula 500 series. Charles had been an amateur racer at Brooklands pre-war, and John was a fairly successful competitor in the new formula, though he soon hung up his helmet to concentrate on the business, which was run from a garage in Surbiton, near London. Coopers became the dominant machines in the low-cost junior series and drivers such as Stirling Moss, Peter Collins, Ken Tyrrell and Bernie Ecclestone all cut their teeth in them.

Easy-going and friendly, John formed a stark contrast to the short-tempered Charles, and the two rowed frequently. Nonetheless, it was John who had the vision and who took the technical concept of the Formula 500 cars and applied it to bigger, faster

▼ John Cooper in 1968.

machinery, until even Formula One surrendered to his funny little cars. His trademark victory somersault at the trackside became very familiar in 1959 and 1960. He later lent his name to the Mini Cooper and stayed in Formula One until 1968, thereafter concentrating on his garage business. He died in 2001.

Ferrari Bite Two Bullets

Ferrari came back with a vengeance in 1961. Preparation was the key to their success. The British constructors had opposed the formula change to 1.5 litres. The governing body had made the change to combat escalating speeds, but the British teams believed it would leave them without suitable engines, thereby effectively handing the competitive advantage to Ferrari, who made their own engines. This became a self-fulfilling prophecy as the British teams failed to make adequate provisions for the formula change, while Ferrari concentrated on readying their new engine and cars.

Ferrari Returns

The subsequent Ferrari 156 was the team's first effort at a proper mid-engined car, and even though its chassis was not as advanced as those already produced by Lotus or even Cooper, its engine was considerably more powerful than the 1.5-litre version

▲ **Phil Hill's Ferrari finished third in the Monaco Grand Prix, Monte Carlo, 1961. It was the start of his title campaign.**

of the Coventry Climax the British teams relied upon. It recalled another of Enzo Ferrari's famous maxims: that he built engines with wheels on.

Only one thing kept the Ferraris from completely annihilating the opposition: the genius of Stirling Moss. In the privately-owned Lotus of his entrant Rob Walker, Moss twice beat the Ferraris – at Monaco and Germany. But in championship terms, the contest was between Ferrari drivers Phil Hill and Wolfgang von Trips. Hill won, becoming America's first World Champion after von Trips crashed to his death at Monza in the penultimate round of the championship. Fourteen spectators died with him.

By the end of the year, Coventry Climax had produced a new V8 1.5-litre engine that for 1962 gave Lotus power

▼ **Winner Phil Hill in the Ferrari 156 leads team-mate Wolfgang von Trips at the 1961 Belgian Grand Prix. They led a Ferrari 1-2-3-4.**

parity with Ferrari, enabling their superior chassis technology to give them the winning edge once more.

BRM Triumphant

Stirling Moss had received career-ending injuries at the beginning of the season, and it was Lotus' works driver Jim Clark who assumed his mantle as the accepted number one. Yet it was Graham Hill and BRM who won the 1962 world crown on account of a better reliability record than the Lotus.

It was the culmination of over a decade's effort from BRM, a team

originally set up as a trust funded by contributions from British industry. By this time, however, it was privately owned and rather better organized. The P57 with which Hill won the title was powered by BRM's very own V8 engine. It was this that transformed the fortunes of the team, turning it from a laughing stock to a world beater. Hill's determination played a key part in driving the team forward.

◄ Graham Hill, here wearing a cap featuring the same London Rowing Club colours as his helmet, won the 1962 title.

Technology 1962

Lotus 25

Lotus redefined Formula One technology with the monocoque construction of their 25 model. Instead of a spaceframe of metal tubing clothed with panels, the aluminium shell was load-bearing and tubing was discarded. The monocoque was stiffer and lighter than the spaceframe, and enabled the suspension to work more effectively. It was also far safer in the event of a serious impact. The technique had long been used in aircraft, but this was its first Formula One application. The entire design of the car was

tailored to the compact dimensions of lead driver Jim Clark, with a cockpit just wide enough to accommodate him and no wider. He was also reclined to an almost horizontal driving position of 35 degrees. It all resulted in an impressive cross-sectional frontal area of just 0.37sq m (3.98sq ft), which compared to 0.54sq m (5.81sq ft) for the rival Ferrari car of 1962.

◄ The gearbox and exhaust end of the revolutionary Lotus 25, the pacesetter of Formula One from 1962–65.

◄ The 25 unclothed, showing just how tightly it was tailored around Jim Clark's dimensions. Chapman confers.

▲ Jim Clark giving the thumbs-up after taking his Lotus 25 to victory in the 1963 Dutch Grand Prix, on his way to the title.

Clark Becomes the Master

T he combination of the Lotus 25 and Jim Clark could not be denied indefinitely, and in 1963 they stormed to victory in seven of the World Drivers' Championship's ten rounds. Frequently their level of performance reduced the rest to bit-players: in the Dutch Grand Prix, Clark lapped the field; in France he led from start to finish, despite a couple of broken valve springs. If he failed to win, it was usually because something in the car broke.

Clark and Chapman

Scotsman Clark had formed a symbiotic relationship with Lotus boss, Colin Chapman. Here was the greatest driver of his era working in harmony with the greatest designer. Few doubted that all records would succumb to the pairing.

It did not always go to plan, however. In 1964, some of the unreliability bugs returned and John Surtees was waiting to pounce. The

▲ Jim Clark (*left*) and Colin Chapman, arguably the greatest pairing of driver and designer ever seen in Formula One.

▼ Jim Clark takes victory in the 1965 French Grand Prix at Clermont Ferrand in his Lotus 33, an update of the 25 model.

Shapers

Colin Chapman

Widely cited as the greatest Formula One designer of all time, Colin Chapman's Lotus cars repeatedly took Formula One technology down new roads, leaving the rest to follow in the dust trails of his fertile mind.

He set himself up as a secondhand car trader while studying engineering at London University, and later designed, and competed in, a trials car based on a pre-war Austin 7, dubbed a "Lotus". While training as a pilot in the Royal Airforce, Chapman built a circuit racer for 750 Motor Club events. So successful was he with it that he took orders for replicas; Lotus, the cutting edge of Britain's Formula One invasion, was born.

The success of the business meant that Chapman had to withdraw from racing cars himself, though his driving

talents were considerable. He was even given a drive in the 1956 French Grand Prix by Vanwall, and was quick in practice but a non-starter in the race after damaging his car.

Colin Chapman died from a heart attack in 1982, aged 54. Everyone who worked with him attests to his enormous charm, yet for each of these stories there's another telling of a hard, and ruthless edge. In business, as in car design, he would always search for the loophole, and this trait left his memory tarnished by his involvement in the DeLorean Motor Company scandal of the early 1980s.

◀ Chapman, here sitting in the Lotus 25, frequently took technology from elsewhere and applied it to Formula One.

former motorcycle champion had begun his Formula One career at Lotus but was now at Ferrari, where he helped hone a new V8 machine, and clinched the title in the final round after Clark's oil pipe came adrift. Surtees remains the only man to have won world titles on two wheels and four.

Clark and Lotus re-established themselves in 1965, the final year of the 1.5-litre formula. They won six of the nine races they contested on their way to both the Drivers' and the Constructors' titles, missing one round in order to compete in the Indianapolis 500 in America. They won that too!

▼ (left) John Surtees, 1964 World Champion for Ferrari. Surtees was already a multiple world title winner on motorbikes when he began his Formula One career.

▼ (right) Surtees' 1964 season came alive with victory in that year's German Grand Prix around the 14 mile Nürburgring.

Return to Power

Formula One cars were given their power back in 1966, with the inauguration of a new 3-litre formula. The 1.5-litre regulations had run their allotted time, and there was a hope from the governing body of tempting the American car manufacturers into the sport, to make it appeal more genuinely to a global audience.

Factories Stay Away

Already a Japanese company, Honda, had entered Formula One and had won the final race of the old formula, at Mexico in 1965. Those who controlled the sport hoped this might herald the return of full factory participation in Grand Prix racing. But it was not to be. Whilst Honda produced some

▲ Jack Brabham's 3-litre Brabham BT19 leads Jim Clark's 2-litre Lotus 33 in the 1966 Dutch Grand Prix at Zandvoort.

▲ Denny Hulme, 1967 World Champion, driving for Brabham. A solitary figure, he retired from Formula One in 1974.

◄ Race winner Jack Brabham leads the Coopers of John Surtees and Jochen Rindt in the 1966 German Grand Prix.

▼ Hulme leads Clark and Brabham on the first lap of the 1966 Dutch Grand Prix. Clark led, but later suffered a car problem.

▼ Jim Clark, Lotus 49, won first time out with the brand new Ford DFV engine, at the Dutch Grand Prix, Zandvoort, 1967.

exceptionally powerful engines, their chassis technology was a long way behind the established top teams, and their success was very sporadic.

The "garagiste" era initiated by Cooper in the late 1950s had made Formula One such a specialized exercise, far removed from road-car production, that a factory could no longer expect to come in and immediately dominate. Although Cooper themselves were, by now, a spent force, their influence was everywhere – in the format of the

teams doing the winning and in the offshoots created directly from Cooper.

The Cooper Legacy

Jack Brabham, Cooper's former lead driver, won the world title for a third time in 1966, this time driving a Brabham car. He was not the only ex-Cooper driver to incorporate the lessons learned there and set up on his own either: Bruce McLaren had done the same thing and would win McLaren its first Grand Prix in 1968.

But a major manufacturer, Ford, did become involved. The European off-shoot of the American car giant funded the development of a new Formula One engine from Cosworth of Britain, the DFV. Labelled as a Ford, this motor would fill the role of providing off-the-shelf Formula One horsepower previously taken by Coventry Climax. It debuted in the Lotus 49 of 1967, and instantly proved the class of its field, but early unreliability let the title slip to the Brabham of Denny Hulme.

Technology 1967

Cosworth DFV

Keith Duckworth, in partnership with Mike Costin, formed Cosworth Engineering in 1958. The company made its name with some devastatingly successful racing engines in the junior formulae, often based on Ford production units.

Helped by a £100,000 investment from Ford, Duckworth designed the V8-cylinder DFV (double-four-valve). It was probably the first Formula One engine designed with the dimensions of the car specifically in mind, and not only was it decently powerful, with an initial 405bhp, but it was also small, relatively light and could be packaged very efficiently. It was also made sufficiently stiff that it could be mounted in such a way that it formed

part of the car's rigidity. This helped the suspension to do its job.

It won first time out, with Jim Clark in the 1967 Dutch Grand Prix, and won for the final time in 1983, in narrow valve-angle DFY form, in the back of Michele Alboreto's Tyrrell at Detroit. It took over the role of the standard Formula One engine and totalled 155 Grand Prix wins to become the most successful of all time. It was one of the most important parts of the matrix of specialist suppliers that allowed the British race car community to thrive and dominate Grand Prix racing.

◄ Keith Duckworth, designer of the revolutionary Cosworth DFV engine, looking at his handiwork, 1967.

Making a Lethal Game Safer

T he long-overdue safety movement in Formula One truly began one wet afternoon in June 1966, when Jackie Stewart suffered a terrifying accident in the first lap of the Belgian Grand Prix, from which he was fortunate to emerge with his life.

Stewart's Great Escape

The Spa-Francorchamps circuit, nestled in a forested Ardennes valley, always featured changeable weather and though the track was dry as the race began, when the leaders first arrived at Malmédy some miles down the road, they were confronted with a sudden downpour. Eight drivers spun, some of them many times. Among them was Stewart, whose BRM overturned in a ditch after striking a stone wall. Trapped inside and with petrol from the tanks leaking down onto him, Stewart was convinced the car's hot exhausts were about to trigger a fire.

With no marshals at the scene, he was rescued by fellow drivers Graham Hill and Bob Bondurant, who had to borrow a spanner from a spectator in order to remove the steering wheel to facilitate Stewart's exit from the car. It then took 20 minutes for an ambulance

to arrive. As an illustration of how little forethought was being given to driver safety, it was horrific.

Stewart's Crusade

From that moment and for the rest of his career, Stewart fought tirelessly for improved safety standards, and was highly unpopular with race organizers, circuit owners – and even some fellow drivers – for doing so.

▲ A cigarette-wielding fire marshal douses the Cooper T86B of Brian Redman, following a high speed accident at Spa in 1968.

▼ (left) The Spa track of the mid-1960s shows the lethal proximity of houses and solid objects.

▼ (right) Richie Ginther's 1961 Ferrari 156 with roll-over bar; but Ginther still wears just a T-shirt instead of fireproof overalls.

The wearing of helmets had only been compulsory since the beginning of 1952, and since then there had been very little safety progress. Seatbelts had not had universal take-up as many drivers feared being trapped by them in a burning car. The wearing of fireproof overalls only came into vogue in the late 1960s, around the time that the first full-face helmets began to appear – though many drivers still opted for open-facers in the following years, showing how difficult change was.

Standards began to improve in car construction. The 1969 regulations stipulated compulsory on-board fire extinguisher systems and sealed rubber bag fuel cells within the tanks. These were the first safety regulations since the introduction of cockpit roll-over bars in 1961.

But the biggest struggle was with circuit owners. It came down to a Stewart-led drivers union – the Grand Prix Drivers' Association (GPDA) – to act militantly and demand changes. Trees were felled from trackside locations, Armco barriers were erected, barbed-wire fencing cleared, marshal training improved, and circuit medical facilities upgraded. Eventually, medical helicopters would be present every time the cars ran, ready to ferry injured drivers to hospital. In time, some venues – notably the public road circuit of Spa-Francorchamps where Stewart had crashed in 1966 – were deemed too dangerous and fell from the calendar.

The changes helped, but the sport remained lethally dangerous. In the 1960s, 12 drivers and 16 spectators were killed in Formula One events. Several more Grand Prix drivers died competing outside of Formula One, notably the great Jim Clark, who was killed in a Formula Two race at Hockenheim shortly after breaking Fangio's all-time record of Grand Prix victories. He had racked up win number 25 in South Africa on New Year's Day 1968. Even the world's greatest driver could become a victim.

◄ Monaco had one of the worst safety records in Formula One during the 1960s. Lorenzo Bandini died here in 1967, the flames from his car fanned by a helicopter taking film footage.

▼ *(left)* There was scant protection for the spectators, let alone the drivers. Sixteen spectators were killed during Formula One races of the 1960s.

▼ *(right)* Lotus mechanics look on at the remains of the Lotus 49B of Jackie Oliver, after he crashed in practice in France in 1968 as a result of aerodynamic turbulence.

Money Talks

Commercial sponsorship hit Formula One in 1968, when Imperial Tobacco plastered their Gold Leaf brand livery over the Team Lotus cars. Until this time, such a practice had been restricted to American national racing, while Formula One teams had plugged only trade backers, with small stickers for tyre, fuel, oil or brake brands in exchange for a free supply of their wares. The Lotus deal took things onto a different scale entirely.

Advertising Enters Formula One

The competitive push of the teams, notably Lotus' Colin Chapman, had led them to pressure the governing body to relax restrictions on commercial advertising on the cars in order to give them bigger budgets for development and design. This duly happened at the end of 1967, and Lotus were the first to take advantage. National racing colours – something first established in the 1900 Gordon Bennett competitions – soon became a thing of the past. Ferrari were an exception, though team boss Enzo Ferrari was able to show disdain for the new trend only because his team had been acquired by motor giant Fiat in 1969, giving financial security but retaining Enzo's autonomy. He was now able to get back to full strength.

▶ **Winner Graham Hill clutching his Monaco trophy, 1968. The victory put him into a firm lead of the championship.**

▲ **Race winner Graham Hill in the Lotus 49B made it four wins around the Principality. Monaco Grand Prix, 1968.**

Life After Clark

Lotus bounced back from the death of Clark, largely thanks to the grit and determination of Graham Hill. With team boss Colin Chapman devastated, Hill took the initiative and in winning the very next Grand Prix following Clark's death, helped the team recompose itself. That was in Spain and in winning the following event in Monaco too, Hill put himself and Lotus in command. Nonetheless, to win the fight they had to fend off two very serious challenges: Jackie Stewart in

▼ **By winning the 1968 Spanish Grand Prix immediately after the death of team-mate Jim Clark, Graham Hill helped Lotus recover.**

the new Matra and reigning champ Denny Hulme in the McLaren. All three contenders were powered by the Ford Cosworth DFV engine.

Stewart's French-built and designed Matra was run by his former Formula Three entrant, Ken Tyrrell, as the pair re-established their partnership to form what would become one of the sport's golden liaisons. Their first victory came in Holland that year but their greatest was at the Nürburgring in a wet and foggy German Grand Prix. Stewart won by over four minutes in one of the greatest performances ever seen around the formidable 14-mile circuit. Hulme won the next two events, with Stewart again on top in the penultimate race. Going into the final round, in Mexico, it was a three-way title shoot-out between Hill, Stewart and Hulme.

Hulme was an early retirement as the race developed into a thrilling dice at the front between Hill and Stewart, with the pair passing and re-passing. Eventually, falling fuel pressure began to lose Stewart power, enabling Hill, Lotus and Gold Leaf to win the race and the Championship. Hill's grit had got the job done once again.

▲ Bruce McLaren (McLaren-Cosworth M7A) finished in sixth place at the USA Grand Prix, Watkins Glen, in 1968.

▲ Bruce McLaren (McLaren M7A) leads Jackie Oliver (Lotus 49B) at the Mexican Grand Prix, Mexico City in 1968. McLaren finished second and Oliver third.

▼ Johnny Servoz-Gavin (Matra MS10) crashed out on lap 71 of the Canadian Grand Prix, Mont-Tremblant, in 1968.

Downforce: The Genie Escapes

At the 1968 Monaco Grand Prix, the Lotus 49 appeared in revised "B" trim. On either side of the nose were two small wings, while the rear bodywork featured an upsweep designed to provide similar download at the rear. The concept of downforce had arrived in Formula One, heralding a completely different scale of performance. It has been with the sport ever since. By the next race, at Spa, Ferrari and Brabham appeared with devices that took the principle a step further, featuring full-width rear wings, separate from the body, mounted direct to the gearbox. Chris Amon took pole position in the Ferrari by the huge margin of 3.7 seconds.

Aerodynamic Technology

The principle essentially involved taking an aerofoil shape, as used for aircraft wings, and turning it upside down so that it provided downforce instead of lift. If air is forced to travel a longer distance over a lower surface than an upper one, it creates a pressure that will force the car to the ground, through the medium of the tyres. In this way, braking and cornering capacity is increased hugely.

Mounting the wings higher up on the car got them out of the disturbed

▲ Jochen Rindt's Brabham BT26 in the 1968 Canadian Grand Prix shows the ugly and dangerous heights wings had reached.

▼ Chris Amon drives the Ferrari 312 to second place in the British Grand Prix at Brands Hatch in 1968.

▼ Graham Hill climbs from his wrecked Lotus after an accident caused by wing failure. He was saved by the retaining barrier.

airflow created by the car itself, and within just a few races, almost all the cars were running front and rear wings mounted on hugely high stalks, feeding the loads directly into the suspension. Teams also began to experiment with wings that could be retracted on the straights to overcome the straightline speed penalty of their drag. It all made for a bizarre spectacle – and a highly dangerous one.

Wings of Unreason

At the Spanish Grand Prix of 1969, Graham Hill crested a rise in his Lotus, and his rear wing snapped off its mounts. Suddenly shorn of its downforce, the car became airborne and crashed heavily. As Hill was making his way back to the pits to get the team to warn his team-mate Jochen Rindt, the sister car suffered exactly the same failure over the same crest, and cannoned off Hill's abandoned wreck. Rindt was trapped in the car but fortunately had suffered only a broken nose. It was a miraculous escape for both drivers, not to mention the spectators. The governing body decided

it had to act, and at the next Grand Prix it banned wings outright. After a subsequent meeting with constructors, a compromise was reached; wings were allowed once more, but no longer could they be either movable or mounted to the suspension. Less effective fixed wings mounted only to the bodywork were allowed, with dimensions and height drastically reduced.

Amid all the controversy, Jackie Stewart and his Ken Tyrrell-run Matra-Ford glided from one immaculate victory to another on the way to their first World Championship. Jochen Rindt was the only one to consistently challenge them, but his Lotus lacked reliability. The Ford Cosworth DFV engine took victory in every single race with Matra, Lotus, Brabham and McLaren cars.

▲ Remarkably Jochen Rindt escaped from this wing failure-induced accident with just a broken nose. It led to wing restrictions.

▲ The remains of Hill's Lotus 49B after his 1969 Spanish Grand Prix accident. He broke a leg in the US Grand Prix later that year.

▲ Jackie Stewart, in car, and Ken Tyrrell pose for some publicity shots for a brand of whiskey at the Canadian Grand Prix, 1969.

The Stewart Years

Jochen Rindt and Jackie Stewart were widely acknowledged as the world's two best drivers as the new decade began. But their competitive circumstances were about to change. Matra, now backed by Chrysler France, could not be seen running Ford engines and so the arrangement with Stewart and Tyrrell came to an end. While making plans to have his own machine built for the following year, Tyrrell purchased a car from a manufacturer new to Formula One, March, for the 1970 season. Unfortunately it wasn't up to the task of sustaining a championship challenge.

◄ Jackie Stewart *(left)* with Jochen Rindt at the British Grand Prix, Brands Hatch in 1970. Rindt was later made Posthumous World Champion of 1970.

▼ Rindt, in the Lotus 72C, wins his fourth Grand Prix in a row at Hockenheim, Germany, in 1970.

A Brutal Season

Jochen Rindt, by contrast, found himself behind the wheel of a new Lotus, the 72, that moved the technical goalposts of Formula One and gave him a real advantage. After a stunning win at Monaco in the old 49 model – where he pressured race leader Jack Brabham into running wide and hitting the barriers on the last lap – Rindt took up residence in the 72 and reeled off four successive victories. Although he was not to know it, these effectively secured him the World Championship crown. Rindt was killed practising for the Italian Grand Prix, through a suspected wheel hub failure. In the remaining four races, no-one overhauled his points score and he became the sport's only posthumous World Champion.

It had been a particularly brutal season, with Piers Courage and Bruce McLaren also killed. With his friends being slain around him, Stewart worked harder than ever on his safety campaign. But he still found time to dominate the 1971 season in his new Tyrrell-Ford, with which he won six races.

The five he didn't win were split between his own team-mate François Cevert, the Ferraris of Mario Andretti and Jacky Ickx, and the Yardley Cosmetics-sponsored BRMs of Jo Siffert and Peter Gethin. The latter triumphed in Italy, where his race average of 241km/h (151mph) is still the fastest recorded in a Grand Prix. Thereafter chicanes were installed in the super-fast Monza track for reasons of safety.

▼ Winner Peter Gethin (BRM, *right*), Ronnie Peterson (March) and François Cevert (Tyrrell) at the Italian Grand Prix, 1971.

Technology 1970

Lotus 72

While the advent of wings in 1968 made Formula One cars substantially faster round a circuit on account of their vastly improved braking and cornering capabilities, the aerodynamic drag they created actually made the cars slower on the straights than before. The 1970 Lotus 72 – conceived by Colin Chapman, translated into reality by Maurice Phillippe – brilliantly resolved the conflicting requirements of downforce and straightline speed.

Its wedge shape made the cigar-like structures of before obsolete. This, combined with the re-siting of the radiators from the front to the side of the car, lowered the frontal area while the wedge bodywork itself helped create downforce. This enabled smaller wings to be fitted for equivalent downforce; powered by the same Ford Cosworth DFV engine, the 72's terminal speed was 14km/h (9mph) higher than the 49's, its predecessor. Other novelties included inboard brakes front and rear to lower the car's unsprung mass, and

rising-rate suspension to resolve the requirements that the very different aerodynamic loadings of high- and low-speed corners placed upon it.

▲ The launch of the Lotus 72 in 1970. The radical car took a few races to be fully sorted but it was devastating thereafter. It was still winning in 1974.

New Eras Beckon

The seeds that eventually flowered to make Grand Prix racing one of the biggest sports in the world were planted some time in 1971. Jack Brabham had retired from racing at the end of 1970 and, at the age of 44, he sold up and went back home to Australia. Initially his designer Ron Tauranac took over the reins of the Brabham team, but later in 1971 Bernie Ecclestone – the late Jochen Rindt's manager – also bought into it.

Big Business

It gave the Brabham team a new lease of life, but very few at the time realized the enormous implications for the future of Formula One. Ecclestone's ownership of a team made him party to business dealings with the race organizers, whom he felt were exploiting the teams. As an incredibly astute businessman, he banded the teams together and negotiated on their behalf. The much-improved deal he secured them was just the start. He also had the vision to see the true business

▲ Bernie Ecclestone (*left*, with Brabham designer Gordon Murray) brought a new era to Brabham – and to all of Formula One.

▼ Emerson Fittipaldi winning the 1972 British Grand Prix at Brands Hatch, on his way to becoming the youngest champ.

potential of Formula One to international sponsors, and so set about securing worldwide television coverage.

Fittipaldi and Lotus

On the track, Emerson Fittipaldi became the youngest-ever World Champion when he clinched the 1972 title at the age of 25 years, eight months and 29 days. The livery of his Lotus 72 had been changed from Gold Leaf to the black and gold colours of John Player Special cigarettes in one of the sport's most distinctive branding exercises. Treadless, "slick" tyres, introduced to Formula One in 1971 but originating from drag-racing, were the norm now, giving a greater surface area of rubber, and therefore more dry-track grip. The combination of downforce and slicks saw cornering forces rise to 2g.

Fittipaldi's Championship campaign had been eased somewhat by Jackie Stewart suffering a stomach ulcer, but for 1973 the Scot came bouncing back to take his third title. At Monaco he scored his 26th Grand Prix win,

breaking the record held by his friend, the late Jim Clark, and at the German Grand Prix he took his 27th and final race victory. At the end of the season, 34-year-old Stewart retired. But at Watkins Glen in the United States, the death of his team-mate François Cevert in practice for what was going to be Stewart's final race, had illustrated that the Stewart-initiated safety campaign had to continue.

▲ *(left)* François Cevert in 1973. The Frenchman perished at the end of the season, on the verge of great success.

▲ *(right)* Emerson Fittipaldi (Lotus) leads winner Jean-Pierre Beltoise (BRM) at Monaco in 1972. It was to be BRM's last victory.

Shapers

Bernie Ecclestone

The Mr Big of modern Formula One started out as just another Formula 500 racer in the early 1950s, combining this with his business of selling second-hand cars and motorcycles in south London. Ecclestone wasn't a bad driver, but his real talent lay in the world of business. He cut his links with the sport after the fatal accident of his close friend Stuart Lewis-Evans in the 1958 Moroccan Grand Prix, and made his fortune in property dealing.

He returned as the business manager of Austrian driver Jochen Rindt in the late 1960s. Rindt was killed at Monza in 1970, but Ecclestone this time stayed around and bought into the Brabham team, following the retirement of its founder Jack Brabham. From that time

onward, Ecclestone almost single-handedly transformed Formula One into a big business and, eventually, one of the biggest sporting series in the world. In the process, he made most of the team owners extremely wealthy, and himself even more so.

Along the way, Ecclestone's Brabham team gave Nelson Piquet world titles in 1981 and 1983, though Ecclestone sold the team in 1987. As head of the Formula One Constructors' Association (FOCA), he continues to wield enormous – some would say ultimate – power in the sport.

◄ Bernie Ecclestone, Brabham owner, at the South African Grand Prix in 1972. Big changes were coming.

The Ferrari Renaissance

Ferrari were badly in the doldrums by the end of 1973. They had just suffered an appalling season in which they never came close to winning a race, and they hadn't been World Champions since John Surtees' triumph of 1964. The top British teams with their "garagiste" kit-cars, using bought-in components, had basically run rings around the Italian thoroughbreds, with their exclusive self-made engines, for the best part of a decade. It was time for a reorganization.

Ferrari Revamps

Enzo Ferrari took the bull by the horns. He made wholesale changes to his technical team, and recruited a new driver line up. A brilliant young lawyer with close family ties to Fiat's Agnelli family, Luca di Montezemolo, was put in charge of the day-to-day running of the team, while Mauro Forghieri was made head of Formula One development. He toiled away to produce the 1974 312B3 model. Distribution of masses

▲ *(left)* Ferrari designer Mauro Forghieri and Niki Lauda in 1974, the two driving forces behind Ferrari's success.

▼ The new Ferrari 312T of Clay Regazzoni *(left)* alongside the previous 312B3 model in the pits at the South African Grand Prix, Kyalami, in 1975.

was his theme. The powerful flat-12 engine – used since 1970 – already brought the centre of gravity down low. Forghieri now set about centring the masses of the car as much as possible too, to make it more manoeuvrable. To this end the cockpit and fuel cells were moved forward within the wheelbase.

Concurrently, Ferrari signed a promising young Austrian driver, Niki Lauda. His technical feedback and appetite for endless hours of pounding round Ferrari's new Fiorano test track pleased Forghieri immensely. Together, they made the 312B3 1974's fastest car – as Lauda's nine pole positions testified. Some impetuosity on Lauda's part, and the occasional glitch from the car, handed the title to Emerson Fittipaldi and McLaren. But for 1975 there would be no such weaknesses as Lauda and Ferrari annihilated the opposition with the new 312T model. After a gap of 11 years, Ferrari were once again on top of the world.

► Winner Emerson Fittipaldi, in the
McLaren M23, at the Canadian Grand Prix,
Mosport Park, in 1974.

▼ (right) Winner Emerson Fittipaldi, in the
McLaren M23, leads second-placed Niki
Lauda at the Belgian Grand Prix at Nivelles,
in 1974.

▼ (left) Emerson Fittipaldi, the 1974
World Champion, driving for McLaren.

Technology 1975

Ferrari 312T

The 312T was the car that broke a
seven-year Championship-winning
streak for Ford Cosworth DFV-powered
machines. It was the masterpiece of
Ferrari's chief designer Mauro Forghieri.

At the car's heart was Forghieri's
flat-12 cylinder engine, which had first
appeared in 1970. With the cylinders
arranged in two horizontally-opposed
lines of six, it had a lower centre of
gravity than the vee-cylinder formation
of the DFV, which benefited handling.
With 12 smaller cylinders, it also had
a greater combustion chamber area,
lower inertia and fewer heat losses,
allowing it to rev higher and produce
more power. But 12 cylinders also
meant it was heavier and thirstier. With
495bhp, it had around 35bhp more
power than a DFV of the time, but was
25kg heavier and had to carry an extra
20kg of fuel at the start of a race.

The innovation of the Ferrari 312T
was Forghieri's transverse gearbox.
This further centralized the masses of
the car, and enabled its handling to be
more responsive. Forghieri also opted
for the maximum width allowed by
the regulations which meant
more frontal area but
brought a twofold
advantage: firstly,

centre of gravity was lowered further;
secondly, it facilitated wide but short
fuel tanks, which allowed a short
wheelbase despite a long engine,
thereby getting around a key drawback
of a 12-cylinder engine, to the benefit
of the car's direction-changing ability.

▼ Clay Regazzoni won twice in the
312T in 1975 and 1976, as support
to team leader Niki Lauda.

The Greatest Story Ever Told

After a fiery mid-season accident, Niki Lauda came back from the dead to fight for the 1976 World Championship, a contest that went down to a dramatic final round in the rain and mist of Japan, overlooked by the menacing Mount Fuji. Lauda's rival was an English former public schoolboy, James Hunt, who could have arrived straight out of a comic-strip. Dashing, blond and caring little for convention, his beautiful model wife had left him for film star Richard Burton earlier that season. It all made for the most fantastic story, one that transcended the sport and brought Formula One unprecedented public attention throughout the world.

Lauda vs Hunt
Lauda began the season as he had ended 1975, by winning in dominant fashion. By the time of the German Grand Prix in August he looked comfortably on his way to a second successive title, despite the often brilliant showings of Hunt in the Marlboro-McLaren. But then Lauda crashed, his Ferrari caught fire and he

◄ James Hunt at the South African Grand Prix in 1976, where he took his second successive pole position for McLaren.

▼ James Hunt in the McLaren M23, finished in third place in the 1976 Japanese Grand Prix, securing him the title by one point.

Technology 1977

Renault RS01

When the 3-litre formula was announced for 1966, there was a clause in the technical regulations stipulating that forced-induction engines could be no bigger than 1.5 litres. It was assumed that such a penalty would prevent anyone building a supercharged or turbocharged engine, the costs of which were expected to be exorbitant. Supercharged engines – whereby a mechanically-driven compressor compresses the fuel/air mix into the cylinders, massively increasing the power – had last been seen in Formula One in 1951. But at that time, exotic alcohol-based fuels that kept the extreme internal temperatures in check were permitted. Since 1958, only

▲ The 1.5-litre V6 was very compact, albeit heavy, thanks to ancilliaries needed for the turbo and its cooling.

▼ Jean-Pierre Jabouille gave the RS01 its first race at Silverstone in 1977, qualifying 21st and retiring in the race.

conventional pump-fuel had been allowed. Despite this, Renault reckoned they could make a success of the turbo engine – whereby exhaust gases rather than a mechanical device drive the compressor. In its initial form, the 1.5-litre V6 produced 500bhp – slightly more than most conventional 3-litre engines were giving. As if the engine were not innovation enough, the Renault was also the first Formula One car to feature radial tyres rather than crossplies, courtesy of Michelin.

It would take many years before Renault could make a turbo engine reliable, but when they did, it released previously undreamed-of horsepower and changed the face of Formula One.

was trapped inside. Some fellow drivers pulled him out but he had suffered critical lung damage through inhalation of the flames. For days his life hung in the balance, and he was even granted the last rites. But, remarkably, he made a rapid recovery. Facially scarred, he returned three races later and finished fourth at Monza in one of the most astonishing performances ever seen in any sport.

He pulled out of the final race in Japan after one lap, unwilling to risk his life in conditions of virtually zero visibility. Hunt finished the race third, taking the Drivers' title by one point.

The story was made even better when in 1977 Lauda succeeded in regaining his crown. Better still, one

of his key victories came in Germany, albeit at a different track; his 1976 accident had ensured that the famous Nürburgring – recognized as the most demanding Grand Prix track of all since being built in 1926 – would never again host a Formula One race.

The 1977 British Grand Prix marked a key moment in Formula One history in the form of an unconventional yellow car that qualified only 21st fastest. It was the first Grand Prix start in 69 years for Renault. More significantly, it signified the arrival in Formula One of turbo-powered engines.

◀ The battle-scarred Niki Lauda returned to retake his World Championship title in 1977, and then he promptly left Ferrari.

The Magic of Ground Effect

The Lotus 78 of 1977 had a magic trick within it, one that took Formula One technology down a new road and would soon increase grip exponentially. In the process, it enabled the band of British constructors that had dominated Formula One for two decades to have a fighting chance against the return of the factories that Renault's entry to the sport now represented.

Lotus Innovations

With the 78 model, Lotus brought the concept of "ground effect" to Formula One. When air is funnelled through a small aperture that then opens out into a wide expanse, it creates a negative pressure. Give this area a seal with the ground and it will suck down. This in essence is how the Lotus worked, giving it a big grip advantage over its closest rivals.

Only car unreliability kept Mario Andretti from comfortably winning the 1977 World Championship with the Lotus 78. For 1978, the Lotus 79 represented an evolution of the concept, and this time the performance advantage it brought was massive. Andretti's only rival for the world crown was his team-mate Ronnie Peterson, but Peterson was contracted to be in a support role to Andretti,

▶ **American racing legend, Mario Andretti, won the 1978 World Championship using the ground-effect Lotus 78 and 79 models.**

▲ **Swede Gunnar Nilsson won the 1977 Belgian Grand Prix in the ground-effect Lotus 78. He died from cancer in 1978.**

and on a couple of occasions finished a dutiful second to him when he could conceivably have passed.

Andretti clinched the title at the Italian Grand Prix, but it was in tragic circumstances. Peterson died as a result of injuries sustained in a startline collision. His car slid beneath a barrier in the force of impact, breaking one of his legs. He was hospitalized but died later that evening from a brain embolism triggered by the broken bone. It was a tragic end to Lotus' glorious season.

▼ **Andretti winning the 1977 Italian Grand Prix in the Lotus 78. Its slow straightline speed was corrected in the 79 model.**

▲ The aftermath of the first lap crash which claimed the life of Ronnie Peterson at Monza on 10 September, 1978.

▶ Ronnie Peterson tragically succumbed to his Monza injuries after a fine season. He was lying second in the Championship.

Technology 1978

Lotus 79

The previous year's Lotus 78 had been the first Formula One car to utilize ground effect. Contained within its side pods were venturi channels, small apertures opening out into a bigger area. When air flowed through these, channels it created a negative pressure, which was sealed off via skirts running along the bottom of the pods, thereby sucking the car to the ground.

The problem with the 78 model was that the centre of pressure was too biased towards the front of the car, necessitating a bigger rear wing to balance the handling, at the cost of straightline speed. In its layout, the 79 addressed this problem, and more fully exploited the potential of the concept. Quite by chance, ground effect also

brought the decade-old Cosworth DFV engine back into play as the most suitable engine for the job. Since the mid-1970s, Ferrari had taken full advantage of the lower centre of gravity endowed by their flat-12 motor to produce the fastest cars in the competition. But efficient ground effect demanded side pods with plenty of open space behind them, in order to

▲ Ronnie Peterson followed Mario Andretti home in the Spanish Grand Prix of 1978, both Lotus 79-propelled.

speed up the airflow and increase the suction. This meant that the cylinder banks of the Ferrari were now in the worst possible place, while those of the DFV, angled upwards in a vee-shape, were perfectly situated.

Safety: Still a Way to Go

R onnie Peterson's fatal accident at the 1978 Italian Grand Prix illustrated just how far there was still to go, over a decade after Jackie Stewart initiated the safety campaign. Peterson was the only Formula One driver to be killed on-track that year, suggesting some improvement since 1970 when three drivers succumbed. But the average for the decade was still slightly more than one driver death per season. The figures also showed that there would be a death or serious injury for every 40 accidents – a big improvement over the 1960s, but still far too high.

Taking Safety Seriously

Professor Sid Watkins, a British neurologist and motor racing fan, had been asked by Bernie Ecclestone to attend some races with a view to making suggestions about how to improve medical facilities. He was present that day at Monza but had no position of authority. His observations of events there indicated many areas where big improvements could be made relatively easily. Soon after,

▲ *(above and inset right)* John Watson in the carbon-fibre McLaren MP4/1, in which he survived unscathed from a huge accident at Monza.

▼ Catch fencing halts the errant cars of Jochen Mass and Nelson Piquet in the 1980 Belgian Grand Prix.

▲ Sid Watkins, FISA Doctor, is swarmed by the Coca-Cola girls at the Brazilian Grand Prix, Rio de Janeiro, in 1981.

▼ Denny Hulme leads Jackie Stewart through a newly-installed chicane at Monza in 1972, designed to keep speeds in check.

Watkins was made chief medical officer for all Grands Prix, which gave him absolute authority. He can bring a meeting grinding to a halt if he is not satisfied with any aspect of safety. The medical facilities of the circuits have since improved immeasurably.

Safety vs Advantage

In terms of car design, new regulations for 1973 stipulated that the space between the monocoque skins had to be filled with hardened foam to provide a deformable structure, and the fuel tanks had to be better insulated. But thereafter, the advent of ground effect cars made it more desirable from an aerodynamic performance point of view to have the cockpits far forward within the wheelbase, even to the extent that drivers' feet were sometimes ahead of the axle line of the front wheels, making them especially vulnerable. A regulation banning this practice didn't come into effect until 1988.

Circuit safety improved throughout the decade. Greater run-off areas were beginning to be provided on the fast corners, tyre barriers were erected, as was catch fencing, which would wrap itself around an errant car and thereby slow its progress. This, however, created a secondary hazard in that the poles to which the fencing was attached could strike a driver's head. The 1980s would see the catch fencing replaced by gravel traps. As a downside to the safety movement, several demanding corners – highlights of the track – were lost from the circuits as chicanes were installed before them to slow cars down to a safer cornering speed.

▲ Safety crusader Jackie Stewart in his post-retirement role of TV commentator talks viewers through a Lotus 79.

▲ Alan Jones and Gilles Villeneuve make use of the catch fencing at the British Grand Prix at Silverstone in 1981.

TV: Spreading the Word

The fairytale story of the 1976 Lauda vs Hunt epic was probably the spark that got television companies interested in Formula One. The British Broadcasting Corporation televised the championship finale – something of a departure from its previous policy of screening the Monaco and British Grands Prix only. In 1978, the BBC began televising every race.

Formula One Goes Global

If Hunt's performances can be said to have been responsible for bringing the BBC in, it was a pattern repeated as drivers of other nations were successful. Australia's Alan Jones began winning races on a regular basis in 1979, triggering Channel Nine's season-long coverage for the following year.

Emerson Fittipaldi's success in the early to mid-1970s saw interest in Formula One soar in Brazil, and the television companies responded appropriately. In each case, the broadcasts were such a success that they remained regular fixtures even after those drivers had left the sport or ceased to be successful. France was an early television convert, thanks to the success of the Elf programme in backing the nation's promising junior drivers until they reached Formula One; by 1978, there were seven French drivers there.

The rights to broadcast Formula One were – and are – negotiated by Bernie Ecclestone. Initially the terms were not too fierce, as he sought to lead them into the sport gently and thereby make it a more attractive place for sponsors

▲ *(left)* James Hunt's 1976 epic title race with Niki Lauda, and his glamorous profile, generated lots of interest from racing fans.

◄ Arguably the dice of the decade unfolded as Gilles Villeneuve and René Arnoux fought over second, France 1979.

▼ Jody Scheckter won the 1979 World Championship after taking his Ferrari to victory three times.

▼ Clay Regazzoni takes the flag at Silverstone 1979 to give the Williams team its first Grand Prix victory.

to be. But steadily, the process snowballed and, as the money rolled in, so the sport became bigger news, and so the fee increased. The television companies happily paid up, as the sport was attracting ever-more television advertising revenue.

Television and Live Drama

By the end of the 1970s, it was all just beginning to take off. There was some particularly good footage to show in 1979, most memorably in the French Grand Prix where Gilles Villeneuve's

Ferrari and René Arnoux's Renault fought one of the most desperate and thrilling wheel-to-wheel battles ever seen, frequently trading rubber or running wide onto the grass in the closing laps of the race. In all the excitement, it was easy to overlook the fact that this was a fight for second place; some way ahead of them, Jean-Pierre Jabouille was himself making a bit of history. In winning the race for Renault, he gave the turbocharged engine its first ever Formula One victory.

At Silverstone for the next race, Clay Regazzoni gave the British Williams team its first win, initiating a lineage of success for them that continues to this day. His team-mate Alan Jones dominated the second half of the season in the ground-effect FW07 model. But it was Ferrari's Jody Scheckter who took the title thanks to three victories and superbly consistent finishing in between.

▼ Clay Regazzoni's Williams in action.

Entente Incordiale: The Battle for Control

Bernie Ecclestone's increasing power and influence through the 1970s had made the sport's nominal governing body, the FIA (Fédération Internationale de l'Automobile), very nervous. When the body elected a new president, Jean-Marie Balestre, in 1978 he vowed that he was going to wrest control of the sport back where it belonged. He included in that mission statement financial control as well as sporting and technical.

David vs Goliath

The body headed by Ecclestone, the FOCA, represented the interests of the independent teams, most of whom were British. It didn't include Ferrari, nor the car-producing factories of Renault and Alfa Romeo, both of whom had recently joined Formula One. Balestre, an outrageously manipulative politician, succeeded in exposing a fault line of conflicting interests between the FOCA and non-FOCA teams.

For 1980, Balestre attempted to ban the sliding skirts used on the sidepods of the cars that were a critical part of their ground effect performance. His stated objection was that they made the cars so much faster that circuits were having to be constantly changed, with ever-greater run-off areas, just to keep pace.

The British constructors, all of them relying on the venerable bought-in Cosworth DFV engine, felt that it was only their superior chassis technology

▲ *(top)* Jean-Marie Balestre, FISA President, talks with Bernie Ecclestone, Brabham team owner and FOCA member.

▼ Jody Scheckter finished second at the United States Grand Prix (West), Long Beach, Florida, in 1979.

▲ *(above)* Pole sitter Nelson Piquet, in the Brabham BT49, took his first Grand Prix win at the USA (West) Grand Prix in 1980.

▼ Max Mosley, March team owner, at the Canadian Grand Prix, Mosport Park, October 1977.

▼ Carlos Reutemann in the Williams FWO7B finished third at the Belgian Grand Prix at Zolder in 1980.

that was preventing Formula One being dominated by a small number of money-no-object factory teams, with their own more powerful engines. The sliding skirts were an essential element to this chassis superiority.

On the Brink of Divide

The argument bubbled on throughout 1980 before the sport split into two camps during the off-season of 1980–81. FOCA announced its own Championship and published a series of dates. Six teams, including Ferrari, Renault and Alfa Romeo, stayed loyal with the governing body, and it looked for a time as if there would be two conflicting World Championships. A South African Grand Prix took place in January with just the FOCA teams. It was a sure recipe for a complete commercial disaster.

Shapers

Jean-Marie Balestre

Noted as bombastic and highly controversial during his time as president of FISA, the sporting arm of the FIA, Balestre did many positive things for the sport during his time at the helm.

After serving in the war as an undercover agent for the French Resistance – posing as a member of the French SS – he established a successful French racing motor magazine, *Autojournal*. He is also given credit for popularizing kart racing, and founded the world karting commission. He rose to a position of authority within French national motorsport and this led to his presidency of the Paris-based world governing body. It was Balestre who established specific crash test requirements for Formula One cars and in so doing raised safety standards enormously. He was re-elected in 1987 and stayed in charge until the 1991 elections when he lost to Max Mosley, who for years had been Ecclestone's key partner in FOCA.

It was a farcical situation and a compromise was finally brokered by Enzo Ferrari. In a meeting at the Ferrari base of Maranello, Balestre and Ecclestone both signed an agreement – called the Concorde Agreement – that is, essentially, the basis on which the sport of Formula One runs today. FOCA was granted the commercial negotiating rights on the FIA's behalf, while the FIA retained control of all sporting and technical regulations.

Many years later Ecclestone revealed that he had been about to telephone Balestre to surrender when Balestre called him to suggest a compromise! At last, the racing could get under-way again, though feelings of distrust between the two sides continued to flare up from time to time.

▼ Jean-Pierre Jabouille, Renault RE20, retired on the first lap with clutch failure. Belgian Grand Prix, Zolder, 1980.

Specialists vs The Factories

Ground effect had arrived just in time to give the British specialist teams a weapon against the exotic turbo engines of the returning factory outfits. It did not take long for Renault to devise their own ground-effect chassis though, and so while the British teams were fighting to have turbos banned, they were also researching avenues through which they could get their own.

On Even Ground

There was a brief window – before Renault had made their engines fully reliable and before the specialist teams had sourced turbos – where a competitive equilibrium between the two was established. That window comprised the 1980 and 1981 seasons.

Alan Jones gave Williams its first World Championship in 1980, pushed hard by the Brabham of Nelson Piquet. The Renaults by now were running close to 600bhp – an advantage of around 100bhp over the DFV cars – and won three races in the hands of René Arnoux and Jean-Pierre Jabouille, but their chassis, despite featuring ground effect, lagged behind those of the best specialist teams and their engines repeatedly blew up.

▲ Alain Prost in the Renault RE30, en route to his first victory and on home soil at the French Grand Prix, Dijon-Prenois, in 1981. It was the first of 51 wins for the Frenchman.

◄ 1980 World Champion Alan Jones retired at the end of 1981 after another great season with Williams. He later returned, but without the same level of success.

▼ Prost's Renault dices hard with Jones' Williams in the 1981 German Grand Prix. It was a classic factory vs specialist team fight: the Renault had superior horsepower, but the Williams had a better chassis.

▼ Nelson Piquet took his Brabham to victory in the 1981 World Championship, defeating the less reliable Renaults.

▼ John Watson took McLaren out of the doldrums with victory in the 1981 British Grand Prix, a first for a carbon-fibre car.

It was a similar story in 1981 when Piquet took his Brabham-DFV to the title, though Alain Prost's Renault was frequently the quickest car and won three times between blow-ups. Ferrari now had their own turbo engine and with it Gilles Villeneuve took two spectacular victories. McLaren, under the new management of Ron Dennis, came back into the reckoning after a few years in the doldrums as John Watson won the British Grand Prix in the MP4/1, the first carbon-fibre Formula One car. Lotus attempted to take ground effect onto the next level with their twin-chassis 88 model, but the governing body banned the car from ever competing.

Technology 1981

McLaren MP4/1

The aerodynamic loads that the ground effect cars put upon their chassis was enormous. The Williams FW07 had been successful because designer Patrick Head had realized that the chassis needed to be massively rigid in order to take full advantage of ground effect forces. But there was a conflict for designers: the bigger the side pod venturis could be made, the more ground effect could be generated; but at the same time, the wider the sidepods, the narrower the central tub of the car, which limited its rigidity.

McLaren designer John Barnard realized the solution would be to make the tub in a material inherently stiffer but no heavier than the widely-used aluminium. Helped by American aerospace supplier Hercules, he made the MP4/1's monocoque from carbon-fibre. Strands of carbon-fibre were laid out into the required shape, bonded together and then oven-baked to make an immensely strong and stiff structure. For the same weight as an aluminium tub, its stiffness was double. It was also much stronger in an impact than

aluminium, as lead driver John Watson demonstrated with an enormous crash at Monza in 1981, from which he improbably climbed out unhurt. Soon, all Formula One cars would be made this way. As with the development of the monocoque chassis in the 1960s, the search for performance had brought with it unexpected benefits in car and driver safety too.

▼ Niki Lauda pilots the MP4/1 McLaren to victory in the 1982 British Grand Prix, his second victory with the car.

Partners Not Enemies

Competitive tension between the specialist teams and the "grandees" (Renault, Alfa and Ferrari) continued into the 1982 season as they fought off-track over the direction the sport was taking, as well as on the track over race victories.

Shady Tactics

Brabham and Williams were disqualified from first and second places in the Brazilian Grand Prix for running their cars underweight. They thought they had identified a loophole in the regulations that allowed them to do this so long as the cars complied when replenishable fluids were added post-race. The ruse they devised were big water tanks for "water-cooled brakes". They ran the race with the water tanks empty, then filled them post-race. It allowed the underpowered DFV-engined cars to run as much as 60kg under the minimum weight, something out of the reach of the turbo-engined machines with their heavy ancillaries. The governing body was not impressed.

Following the disqualification, the FOCA teams boycotted the San Marino Grand Prix. The rules were clarified and both sides were back together in time for the following Belgian Grand Prix. It was in qualifying for this race that Gilles Villeneuve was killed after his

Ferrari hit a slow-moving car, got airborne and crashed nose-first into the ground. The French-Canadian had been favourite to lift the 1982 Championship crown, as the Ferrari's powerful turbo engine was now mated to an efficient British-style chassis, and was generally the fastest car of the year.

▼ Fifth place finisher Derek Daly (*by rear wing*) discusses the demands of the new Detroit circuit as mechanics work on his Williams FW08 at the United States Grand Prix, Detroit, in 1982.

▲ Nelson Piquet (Brabham) (*centre*) was on the verge of collapse at the Brazilian Grand Prix, Rio de Janeiro, in 1982. To add to his woes, both he and second place finisher Keke Rosberg (Williams) (*left*), were subsequently disqualified, leaving Alain Prost (Renault) (*right*) as the eventual race winner.

▼ The Brabham team were embroiled in the "water-cooled" brakes controversy that led to the disqualification of Nelson Piquet (Brabham BT49D) from second place in the 1982 Brazilian Grand Prix.

Achieving Compromise

As it was, Keke Rosberg and Williams gave the old DFV engine its final championship glory as the Renaults again proved insufficiently reliable. But the message was clear: turbos were the future. Bernie Ecclestone's Brabham team had recognized as much and had gone into partnership with BMW, thereby merging specialist constructor chassis expertise with big factory financial and technical resources. It was to prove the way of the future, and the two types of entrant finally found peace as they flourished in Formula One together. The war was over.

As part of their imaginative campaign, Brabham also reintroduced the tactical pit stop to Formula One racing after a 25-year absence. Designer Gordon Murray realized that a low fuel/soft tyre compound car would more than make up for time lost in the pits by greater pace on the track. Soon everyone would be doing it, introducing a new competitive element to the races. Bosch introduced electronic engine management to the BMW engine, a critical step in making the turbo motor reliable, while BMW pioneered car-to-pits telemetry.

In 1983, Piquet took his Brabham-BMW turbo to a final race title showdown with Renault's Alain Prost, and won. The Renault team stuttered on for another two seasons, but those doing the winning (McLaren-Porsche, Williams-Honda) were based on the blueprint of the Brabham-BMW partnership. Many years later Renault would finally win its first World Championship in partnership with Williams. Mutual success for specialists and factories was the new way.

▲ *(left)* Keke Rosberg drove for Fittipaldi, but failed to score any points over the 1981 season.

▲ *(right)* Alain Prost's Renault RE40 took pole position and won on Formula One's return to the Belgian circuit at Spa in 1983.

▼ Nelson Piquet's Brabham-BMW BT52 retired from the German Grand Prix at Hockenheim in 1983.

Changing of the Guard I

S oon after losing out in the 1983 title fight with Nelson Piquet, Alain Prost was sacked from Renault. It came at a moment when McLaren had not finalized who was going to drive their new Porsche turbo-powered car alongside Niki Lauda. Prost was quickly snapped up.

The Emergence of Prost

It was a fortuitous chain of events for Prost because almost by chance it put him into the fastest car of 1984. It soon became clear that the only thing standing between him and his first world title was Lauda in the sister car. Their in-team battles rescued Formula One from what might otherwise have been a dull year, such was the advantage enjoyed by the McLarens.

Lauda, with two World Championship titles to his name, had retired at the

end of 1979, saying he was "bored with driving round in circles". But he could stand only two years away from the cockpit and McLaren's Ron Dennis had lured him back for 1982. He was fourth on his first race back and it took only two more events before he was winning again. Still relying on DFV engines, the McLarens had been outpowered by the turbos in 1983 and Lauda had suffered a barren season. There were those who were wondering if he still had what it took, but in the

◀ Alain Prost in 1984.

▼ Alain Prost's McLaren MP4/2 led the race, but a gearbox failure allowed his team-mate Niki Lauda through to take victory at the British Grand Prix, Brands Hatch, in 1984.

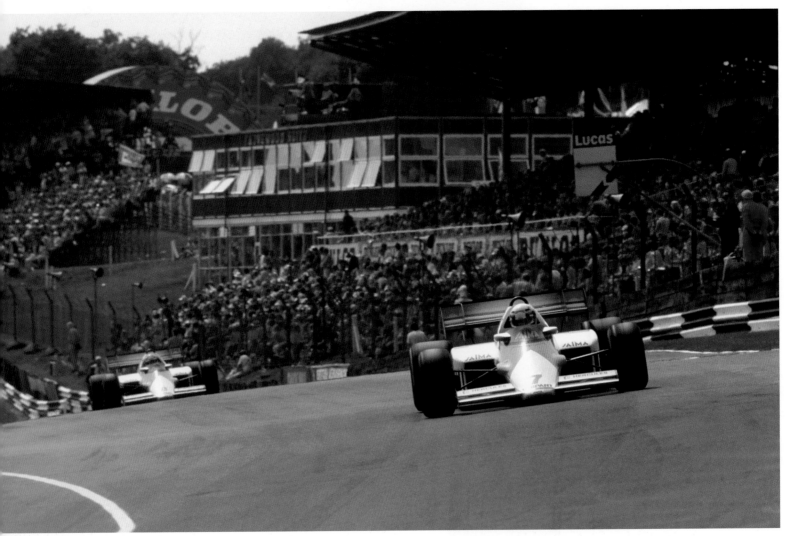

final race of 1983, armed with the turbo, he had driven an extremely strong race, closing down on the leader before his engine expired.

Lauda Holds Off

As the 1984 season progressed, it soon became clear that Prost, as the younger, hungrier man, had a clear edge in speed. But Lauda had the guile and cunning of experience and he put it to superb use. They arrived at Estoril, Portugal, for the final round with nine points up for grabs and Lauda just 3.5 points ahead.

Prost qualified on the front row and quickly established a big lead in the race. Lauda had qualified a disastrous eleventh, and for much of the race was stuck in tenth, making no progress. As cars dropped out ahead, Lauda moved up to seventh. Assuming Prost was going to win this race, Lauda needed to finish second in order to clinch the title. He then began to get a move on, quickly disposing of Johansson, Alboreto and a young driver in his first season, Ayrton Senna. Now Lauda was third, with just Nigel Mansell's Lotus between him and a third world title. Lauda could make no gains on the Lotus, but at around three-quarter distance, Mansell was

suddenly lapping much slower – his brakes were failing. Lauda duly picked him off and cruised to his third title – five years after retiring!

The McLarens retained their dominant form into 1985, but Lauda suffered an appalling reliability record. By contrast, Prost glided from win to win, and took his first title by a comfortable margin. Only in Zandvoort, for the Dutch Grand Prix, was there an echo of 1984, when Lauda resolutely

held off a charging Prost in the closing stages to take his 25th – and final – Grand Prix victory. At the end of the season, Lauda retired once again, and this time he stayed out for good. It was a remarkable end to a remarkable two-part career.

▼ Niki Lauda's McLaren MP4/2B leads second-placed team-mate Alain Prost to take his twenty-fifth and final Grand Prix victory at Zandvoort, Holland, in 1985.

Prost vs Williams

By the tail-end of 1985, with Alain Prost well on his way to winning the title, the pace of the McLaren-Porsches was finally overcome by that of the Williams-Hondas, which won the final three races. For 1986 Williams enlisted double World Champion Nelson Piquet to partner Nigel Mansell, and thus made themselves favourites for the title. But that was to reckon without an intense personal battle between the two Williams drivers – and also the supreme skills of Prost.

The Race for Pace
The McLaren-Porsche successes had been built on a compact, fuel-efficient engine, the specification of which was largely laid down by McLaren designer John Barnard. As a paying customer that had exclusively commissioned the

▲ The Williams-Honda mechanics work on Nelson Piquet's car at the 1986 British Grand Prix at Brands Hatch.

engine from Porsche, McLaren were able to dictate what they needed rather more effectively than Williams, whose engines were supplied free of charge by Honda.

The Porsche's compact dimensions had allowed Barnard to design an aerodynamically efficient car. Since 1983, ground effect side venturis and skirts had been banned and so the emphasis came back to upper bodywork and maintaining a good balance between low drag and high downforce. Barnard's McLarens were tightly waisted around the engine, giving a healthy airflow to the rear wing of the car.

Fuel stops had been banned since 1984 and a fuel limit of 220 litres imposed. The trick for engine designers was to reach an efficiency level that still allowed a reasonable amount of turbo boost to be used. In this, the Bosch electronic control of the Porsche was supreme, and very much key to McLaren's world titles of 1984 and 1985. By 1986, however, Honda had caught up – and even surpassed – Porsche in this respect. Their engines were giving over 900bhp for the races and an astounding 1200bhp in high-boost qualifying trim. Williams had also begun to use the underfloor of the car,

◀ The dominance of the Williams-Hondas in 1987 was emphasized at the British Grand Prix. They were over a lap clear at the end.

▼ Nelson Piquet's Williams FW11B leads at the start of the 1987 Austrian Grand Prix at the Osterreichring. He finished second.

aft of the regulated flat-bottom area that extended to the rear axle line, to create more downforce. A sharp upwards sweep of the underbody formed a "diffuser" that created ground effect.

The Guile of Prost

Williams' year got off to a terrible start even before the season began as team boss Frank Williams was crippled in a road accident. He missed most of the year as designer Patrick Head stepped up to run the show. Mansell and Piquet fought like demons, fuelled by an intense dislike of each other. Prost's car wasn't usually as fast, but he won whenever the Williams faltered and sometimes – such as at Imola and Monaco – he simply out-drove and out-thought the Williams drivers. Going into the final round at Adelaide, Mansell had a six point lead. By lap 63, the three title contenders were in the

▶ Nigel Mansell wrestles his Williams FW11 back under control after his rear tyre blew on the Brabham Straight costing him the 1986 World Championship crown.

first three positions in the order of Piquet, Mansell, Prost. If it stayed like this Mansell would be Champion. But with 19 laps to go, Mansell's rear tyre exploded at around 300km/h (190mph). He wrestled the car to a stop, but his title was gone. Piquet was called in for a precautionary tyre change, leaving Prost to win the race and an unexpected second Championship.

The End of Turbo

In 1987, Williams extended their speed advantage over McLaren, and this time the title fight was between Piquet and Mansell, even though in winning the Portuguese Grand Prix, Prost broke Jackie Stewart's record of 27 wins. Piquet won the title after Mansell injured his back in a crash during practice for the penultimate round in Japan.

Changing of the Guard II

In a surprising development, Honda switched its supply of engines for 1988 from Williams to McLaren. As part of the deal, McLaren acquired the services of Ayrton Senna, who had driven a Honda-powered Lotus in 1987. In Senna and Prost, McLaren had possibly the most explosive driver line-up of all time. In Gordon Murray's MP4/4, it also had one of the greatest car designs. The combination produced the most dominant season enjoyed by any team in the modern era of Grand Prix racing. McLaren won 15 of the 16 races comprising the Championship.

It was the final year in which turbocharged engines would be allowed. The governing body had introduced a 3.5-litre non-turbo class in 1987 and then limited the turbos yet further for 1988. They were not allowed to run any more than 2.5-bar boost (it had been limited to 4-bar in 1987) and they had to do a race distance on no more than 150 litres of fuel. For the non-turbo engines there was no fuel limitation. By 1989 the turbos would be outlawed. Controlling costs was put forward as the rationale behind this, but more likely it suited both the manufacturers and appeased the smaller teams, who had been calling for a turbo ban for years.

◀ **Ayrton Senna in 1988.**

▼ **Senna's McLaren MP4/5 prepares to head out on to the track as team-mate Alain Prost waits in the pits.**

▼ Gerhard Berger's Ferrari F187/88C leads team-mate Michele Alboreto to an emotional 1-2 home finish at the Italian Grand Prix, Monza, in 1988.

Although it had been the turbo-charged format that had attracted Renault to Formula One in 1977, and their subsequent success that had enticed other big manufacturers into the sport, those manufacturers had no intention of leaving Formula One just because of a return to normally-aspirated motors. Indeed, turbocharging was beginning to fall out of fashion for road-going engines as a new emissions law loomed, so the change of formula suited them fine. The turbo era had introduced them to Formula One and changed the scale of money in the sport, but its increasing global reach and image had more than justified the investment.

The massive financial investment by manufacturers had allowed the top teams to grow quickly in size and resources. Teams invested in wind tunnels and research and development programmes, and as quickly as new regulations were issued to control performance so new research-led solutions appeared. McLaren and Honda demonstrated as much in 1988 when even with the severe turbo engine restrictions, they dominated and easily eclipsed the non-turbo runners. Resources were now everything.

▲ Enzo Ferrari, racing driver from a different era and founder of the Ferrari marque, photographed c.1983.

Senna vs Prost

Senna clinched the Championship from Prost at the last round. In a parallel to the Lauda-Prost McLaren line-up of 1984, the younger, hungrier Senna was the quicker driver, but Prost had guile. It was an uneasy relationship from the start and would develop into a hostile one the following season.

The only 1988 race not won by McLaren was the Italian Grand Prix, where Senna, leading, was tripped up lapping a backmarker. With Prost already out, it gifted Ferrari a 1-2 result on home soil. Just a few weeks earlier, the team's founder, Enzo Ferrari, had died at the age of 90. He had been the last link to a very different age.

Prost Makes a Stand

he new non-turbo 3.5-litre era made little difference to McLaren and Honda's form. Like the returning Renault, who supplied the Williams team, Honda opted for a V10 engine, judging it the ideal compromise between the all-out power of a V12 and the compact packaging and economy of a V8.

Bitter Inter-team Rivalry

With up to 685bhp, the Honda was the most powerful engine in the field in 1989, leaving Senna and Prost to once again fight for the title. At Imola, the second round of the Championship, the pair fell out over a pre-race agreement not to fight into the first corner. Senna led clearly at the start and Prost didn't force the issue, but then the race was restarted after an enormous fiery accident for Gerhard Berger's Ferrari brought out the red flags. On the restart Prost led cleanly away, but this time Senna forced his way down the inside on his way to winning the race. Prost was furious, and from that moment on the pair were sworn enemies. The advantage see-sawed between them as the season played

out and, into the penultimate round in Japan, Prost was ahead on points. Senna needed to win here to keep the title fight open until the final round. The Frenchman dominated the first half of the race, but gradually Senna began to reel him in. On lap 47, just six from

▲ The moment when Alain Prost and team-mate Senna tangle to a standstill at the Japanese Grand Prix, Suzuka, 1989.

▼ After their collision, Alain Prost walks away mistakenly believing his car had been damaged in the accident.

▼ Senna pits for a new nosecone after his collision with Prost at Japan in 1989. Prost had already retired from the race.

the end, Senna made a move under braking into the chicane from a long way back. Essentially, it gave Prost the choice: either he gave way or had a collision. In no mood for compromises, Prost deliberately turned in on Senna and they tangled. They sat gesturing to each other in their stationary cars before Prost jumped out, falsely believing his machine had suffered suspension damage.

Senna restarted, returning to the track via the escape road, then pitted for a new nosecone, and came back to win the race. But he was subsequently disqualified for his use of the escape road, and the title went to Prost. Senna was furious, as was McLaren team boss Ron Dennis because Prost had already announced he was leaving McLaren for Ferrari in 1990. This result meant he would be taking the number one (reserved for the World Champion), with him. But the war between Prost and Senna was not over yet.

Technology 1989

Ferrari 640

Ferrari came back strongly in 1989, with a radical new John Barnard-designed car that Nigel Mansell and Gerhard Berger took to three victories. Powered by a V12 engine, its biggest innovation was a semi-automatic clutchless gearbox worked by electro-hydraulics.

Gear paddles on the back of the steering wheel – one for up, the other for down the box – replaced the conventional gear lever. It meant the cockpit could be narrower, to the benefit of the aerodynamics, and the mechanism could change the gears

faster than any driver. It also meant the driver could have two hands on the wheel at all times, which on certain types of corner with heavy braking into a tight apex, found him a lot of time.

It was an innovation that was widely copied, and it is now a standard feature of all Formula One cars.

◄ Gerhard Berger was thankful for the Ferrari 640's strength after surviving a huge impact at Imola in 1989.

▼ Berger didn't enjoy quite the same success with the 640 as Nigel Mansell. The car proved quick but unreliable initially.

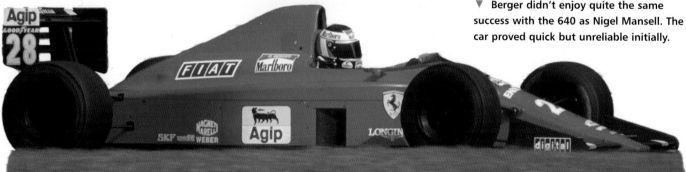

Prost and Senna: War

 he separation of Prost and Senna into separate teams did nothing to dilute the intensity of their battles in 1990. On the contrary, it now gained an even sharper edge. It was a finely-matched season between the two of them. Senna was the world's fastest driver aided by the Honda V10, still the most powerful engine. His nemesis Prost enjoyed the benefits of a Ferrari that was a little down on power but which had a clear handling advantage.

Neck and Neck

Senna began the season strongly, but Prost hit back with three consecutive mid-season victories. One of these, in Britain, was at the expense of his team-mate Nigel Mansell who was commanding the race until his gearbox played up. In an emotional outpouring afterwards, Mansell announced that he was going to retire at the end of the

▲ Ayrton Senna (*left*) and Alain Prost end up in the gravel after their run-in at the Japanese Grand Prix, Suzuka, in 1990.

▼ Senna (*left*) goes down the inside of Prost at Suzuka in 1990 with no intention of lifting off for the looming corner.

▼ Senna (*right*) and Prost walk back to the pits after retiring from the 1990 Japanese Grand Prix.

▼ Ayrton Senna at Monaco in 1991. Victory here was part of a campaign that took him to his third – and final – world title.

year. He was unhappy at the way Alain Prost had walked into what had been Mansell's team and been able to centre it around him.

A win for Prost in Spain made it five victories to the six of Senna, and then came Japan, the scene of their famous altercation the year before. Senna set pole, slightly quicker than Prost. The Brazilian then complained that the grid layout left him on the dirty side of the track, which would make him potentially slower off the line than Prost. He asked that the sides be changed, so he could benefit from his pole position. He was livid when the request was refused.

With this and their accident the year before as a backdrop, Senna had a ruthless plan if, as he feared, Prost was able to out-accelerate him away from the lights. Prost duly got ahead at the start, and the pair of them headed down to the first corner, braking from around 225km/h (140mph). Or at least Prost braked. Senna did not even lift the accelerator, and in a cynical move hit the back of the Ferrari, taking them both off into the gravel trap and retirement from the race. Now, with just one race to go, Prost could no longer catch his rival's points score.

► Winner Nigel Mansell at Silverstone in 1991. He pushed Senna close for the Championship as preparation for 1992.

Senna was World Champion for the second time.

Mansell had since "unretired", having been talked into returning to the Williams team which had enjoyed a promising 1990, with Riccardo Patrese and Thierry Boutsen scoring a win apiece in the improving Renault-engined car. It was a good move: the Ferrari effort imploded in 1991, while the Williams-Renault gradually emerged as the fastest car of all. Mansell was able to push Senna's now V12 Honda-powered McLaren hard, but Ayrton was able to hang on for title number three. After falling into complete disarray, the Ferrari team sacked Prost two races before the season finished for being publicly critical about his car. He took a sabbatical the following year.

Gizmos to the Fore

Williams had followed Ferrari's early lead in developing a semi-automatic electro-hydraulic gearbox in 1991. Their chief aerodynamicist Adrian Newey had also come up with a highly efficient chassis. What Newey wanted to do now was make the next step – active ride. After much haranguing of technical director Patrick Head, Newey was finally given the go-ahead to develop what would turn out to be the dominant machine of 1992.

Active Ride

As long ago as 1983 active ride had been tried by Lotus, but the technology of the control systems of that time were insufficiently sophisticated. In 1987, both Lotus and Williams had won races with active ride cars, but at the time there didn't seem to be enough benefit over conventionally-sprung cars, and the developments were shelved.

By the early 1990s, the control systems were much improved and the cars were more pitch-sensitive than ever before – their aerodynamic effectiveness varied a lot according to the pitch of the car. There was an

▲ Adrian Newey, Williams chief designer, who was responsible for the all-conquering Williams FW14B.

▼ Nigel Mansell, winner of the Brazilian Grand Prix, 1992. Mansell took the FW14B to victory in the first five races that season.

enormous increase in aerodynamic performance to be had by keeping the ride height of the cars constant at all times. Active ride was perfect for this. Instead of springs and dampers, the suspension featured computer-controlled hydraulic actuators that would react in a split-second to the loads put on the car, and keep the ride height constant at all times, eliminating pitch, dive and roll.

The resultant Williams FW14B was a devastating tool. Mansell won the first five Grands Prix of 1992 and took nine victories during the season, both record-breaking statistics. He clinched the world title at the Hungarian Grand Prix, with five races still to go.

Early in 1992 Williams had taken the precaution of signing Alain Prost for 1993, and Prost took over leadership of the team as Mansell failed to agree financial terms and left to go Indycar racing. Mansell was replaced by test driver Damon Hill.

Traction Control

Not only did every serious team have active ride by 1993, but traction control

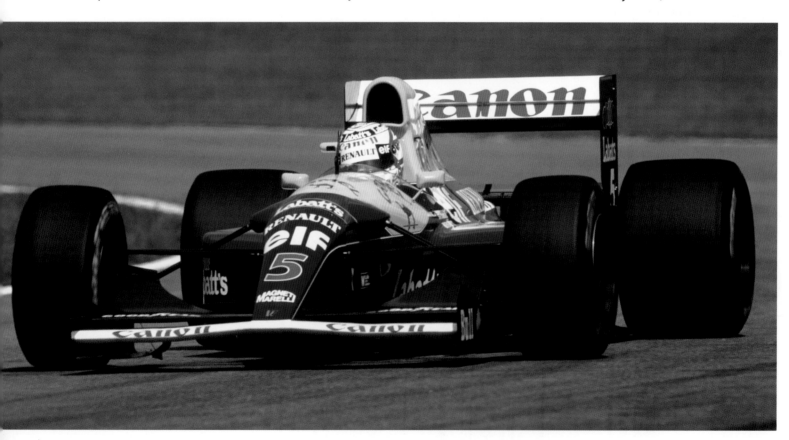

was an almost universal feature too, whereby computers would cut power to the wheels when excessive wheelspin was detected. In some cars, notably the Benetton B193, this system was combined with an automatic "launch control" system; the driver just pressed buttons to "arm" the system, then another as the lights changed and the car would automatically make the optimum getaway. The Benetton also featured four-wheel-steer. Williams introduced anti-lock ABS braking to their cars part-way through the season, while McLaren was working on a programme that, when perfected, would give different chassis settings from corner to corner.

While the other teams may have caught up with Williams in 1993 in the number of electronic gizmos used, the aerodynamic efficiency of the FW15 and the power of its Renault V10 made it by far the fastest car, which enabled Alain Prost to clinch his fourth title fairly comfortably. He took his 51st and final Grand Prix victory at the German Grand Prix at Hockenheim to set a record that would stand for some years. At the end of that season Prost retired.

▲ Damon Hill in the Williams FW15C takes the chequered flag for his first Grand Prix victory at the Hungarian Grand Prix, Hungaroring, in 1993.

◄ Race winner Nigel Mansell at the Mexican Grand Prix, Meixco City, 1992. Mansell set a new world record that year of nine wins in one season.

▼ Race winner Alain Prost in the Williams FW15C at the San Marino Grand Prix, Imola, Italy, in 1993.

The Senna Tragedy

 yrton Senna, the world's greatest driver, was killed live on television on 1 May 1994. Just the previous day, Roland Ratzenberger had perished at the same Imola track. These were the first driver fatalities at a Grand Prix for 12 years. While this emphasized the great safety strides that had been made, the shocking events of Imola shook Formula One into a new safety initiative as the sport's right to exist came under scrutiny in a way unseen since the Le Mans tragedy of 1955.

De-humanizing the Sport

The 1994 season had started on a controversial note with the banning of "driver aids". Traction control, launch control, ABS braking, active suspension, and pits-to-car telemetry that enabled settings to be changed from the pits while the car was on the track, were all deemed illegal. The governing body, headed by Max Mosley, felt that the gizmos were de-humanizing the sport, damaging its public appeal. Concurrently, refuelling pit stops were reintroduced.

Senna, newly signed for Williams-Renault, had struggled in the opening two races against the Benetton-Ford of Michael Schumacher. Ever since making a startling Formula One debut at Spa in 1991, the German had been considered the man most likely to inherit Senna's

▲ **Ayrton Senna in the Williams FW16 follows the painfully slow safety car after the startline crash at the San Marino Grand Prix.**

▼ **Senna embarks on his final lap before tragically losing his life in an accident on lap six at Imola, 1 May 1994.**

▼ Roland Ratzenberger lost his life the day before Senna, at Imola. The Austrian was in his first season of Formula One.

throne as the world's number one. The early races of 1994 confirmed as much as Senna struggled with a car suffering an aerodynamic flaw and lacking the traction and stability of Schumacher's car. The change in regulations appeared to have slowed Senna's car more than Schumacher's.

Death at Imola

Senna was leading Schumacher at Imola when the race came under the jurisdiction of the safety car, soon after the start, in order that debris from a startline accident could be cleared up. Upon the resumption of racing, Senna was pushing extremely hard to keep Schumacher at bay when he lost control through the flat-out kink of Tamburello. He hit the retaining wall

Shapers:

Max Mosley

As President of the sport's governing body, the FIA, since 1991 Mosley has been extremely pro-active on the safety issues of the sport, and has successfully fended off an EEC initiative that threatened to wrest exclusive control of the sport away from the FIA. Through the FIA, Mosely has also initiated a vigorous safety testing procedure for road car manufacturers in an effort to transfer safety lessons learnt in racing to the road.

An urbane lawyer, he is the son of former English Fascist leader, Sir Oswald Mosley. He took up racing in the 1960s, competing as high as Formula Two, and in 1969 he co-founded March Engineering, which entered Formula One the following year. The team won three Grands Prix in the 1970s, and the company became a highly successful customer race car producer.

▲ Max Mosley, President of the FIA. He pushed through extensive safety measures after Imola in 1994.

Mosley was a key member of FOCA, and in the early 1980s fought hard alongside Bernie Ecclestone, wrestling the FIA for control of the sport. The poacher became gamekeeper when he was elected as former foe Jean-Marie Balestre's replacement in 1991.

at around 210km/h (130mph), and a suspension part flew off and pierced his helmet, inflicting fatal injuries.

At the Monaco Grand Prix, where Karl Wendlinger went into a coma following impact with a protective barrier, Max Mosley announced a series of regulation changes to address the safety issue. Stepped-bottom regulations limiting ground effect were imposed from the very next race, together with a pit lane speed limit.

From 1995, engine capacity would be reduced to 3 litres and cockpits had to feature protective raised sides. The FIA's safety programme has been ongoing since the deaths at Imola in 1994, with a series of ever-tougher crash tests and compulsory safety features introduced on a regular basis.

▼ A scorching start helped Michael Schumacher's Benetton to victory in the 1994 French Grand Prix.

Damon's Debacles

Following the death of Ayrton Senna, the 1994 season distilled into a controversial duel between Benetton's Michael Schumacher and Williams' Damon Hill. The German was widely acknowledged now as Formula One's greatest exponent, while the early aerodynamic problems of the Williams were quickly sorted to make it Formula One's fastest car.

Life After Senna

Schumacher had taken victory in the first four rounds before Hill made his seasonal breakthrough, with victory in Spain. Spookily, it echoed his late father Graham's achievement of 1968, when victory at the same race had acted as a much-needed tonic for a team devastated by the loss of its number one driver. Here, Damon did much the same thing for Williams. For all that, Schumacher astonished by finishing second in a car that for much of the race was stuck in fifth gear.

At the British Grand Prix that year, Schumacher was given a draconian race ban for the relatively minor infringement of overtaking on the warm-up lap. This was later changed to a two race ban! Combined with his disqualification from victory in the Belgian Grand Prix – because the underfloor wooden plank, which ensured the regulation stepped-bottom rules were met, had been ground away

▲ Damon Hill (*left*) and Michael Schumacher in the midst of a robust battle for the lead, Belgium, 1995.

◀ Schumacher's professional foul on Hill, Adelaide 1994, ensured the German took his first world title.

▼ Michael Schumacher tries a daring move inside Damon Hill at the 1995 Portuguese Grand Prix at Estoril.

▼ Race winner Michael Schumacher in the Benetton B195 at the 1995 Monaco Grand Prix, Monte Carlo.

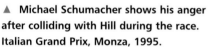

▲ Michael Schumacher shows his anger after colliding with Hill during the race. Italian Grand Prix, Monza, 1995.

when he spun on a kerb – it somewhat artificially made the final round in Australia a title-decider.

Schumacher and Hill quickly pulled away from the rest of the field, both stretching themselves to their very limits. It was Schumacher who cracked first, glancing the wall before rejoining the track. This had happened out of Hill's sight, and as he then made a dive for the inside at the next corner, Schumacher turned in on him and terminally damaged the Williams' suspension. Schumacher was champion

▲ Schumacher discusses tactics with technical director Ross Brawn (centre) and Pat Symonds (left) at Silverstone in 1994.

▼ Schumacher and Benetton completely dominated the 1995 championship, frequently humiliating Hill and Williams.

under the most controversial circumstances in what had been an intensely controversial season.

There was to be no doubting the outcome in 1995 though. Benetton was newly equipped with a Renault engine like that in the Williams, which nonetheless retained its status as Formula One's fastest car. Despite this, Schumacher and the Benetton team consistently out-performed Hill and Williams, taking nine victories on the way to a comfortable title. Schumacher and Benetton technical director, Ross Brawn, repeatedly won races through superior pit stop strategies, as they formed an incredibly close working relationship.

Schuey Joins Ferrari

After winning two consecutive World Championships with a relatively unfancied team, what next was there for Michael Schumacher? It would have been quite straightforward to have negotiated a place at Williams, who had the fastest car and biggest depth of technical talent. It would probably have been the work of a moment to make himself part of Mercedes-Benz's ambitious Formula One plans in partnership with the mighty McLaren team. What he did instead was accept motorsport's biggest challenge: he transferred to Ferrari, the biggest name in Formula One, but a team in disarray that hadn't been a championship contender for years.

▲ Ferrari President Luca di Montezemolo (*left*) and team manager Jean Todt (*right*): architects of the Ferrari revival.

Ferrari Steadies Ship

Scuderia Ferrari had been through some turbulent times since the death of its founder Enzo Ferrari in 1988, but a measure of management stability seemed to arrive following Luca di Montezemolo's appointment as president of the company in late 1991. A man close to the Agnelli family of parent company Fiat, Montezemolo had been Ferrari's Formula One team manager in the 1970s, but since then had risen through the corporate ranks. No longer could he devote his time

▼ Despite an uncompetitive car, Michael Schumacher won three times in the 1996 Ferrari, aided here by the rain at Barcelona.

▼ **Michael Schumacher with Ferrari technical director Ross Brawn (*left*) at the 1997 French Grand Prix at Magny-Cours.**

to the running of the Formula One operation, and for this role he recruited Jean Todt, a man with a brilliant reputation as a team organizer honed first in rallying, then with the Peugeot sportscar squad.

The Long Road to Success

With money no object, Todt wanted the best available and so he recruited Schumacher. What the German found when he arrived was a team still rebuilding. By the standards of a top Formula One team, the on-site technical facilities were lacking. Technical director John Barnard had set up a satellite operation in Britain where he designed and built the cars. When Schumacher tested the new V10-engined F310 model he realized immediately he was in for a difficult season. Its handling was woeful, and its reliability worse. Somehow he managed to win three races with it in 1996, but at no stage that season was he or the Ferrari team in Championship contention. For 1997, Barnard had produced a much better

car but his Ferrari contract was coming to an end. Schumacher pushed to have the team recruit the man with whom he had shared success at Benetton, Ross Brawn. With him came Benetton chief designer Rory Byrne. The triangle was reunited. From that moment, Ferrari just got better.

▲ **Michael Schumacher in the Ferrari F310B took second at the 1997 German Grand Prix.**

▼ **Ferrari's line-up (*left to right*): Paulo Martinelli (engine chief), Michael Schumacher, Ross Brawn (technical director), Jean Todt (sporting director), Rubens Barrichello, and Rory Byrne (chief designer).**

▼ **Michael Schumacher's Ferrari F310B finished second at the San Marino Grand Prix at Imola in 1997.**

Second Generation Champions

With Michael Schumacher struggling in his first year at Ferrari, 1996 represented Damon Hill's best chance yet for a world title, equipped as he was with the latest Williams-Renault model, the FW18.

Damon Comes Good

He made full use of the opportunity with a series of very polished performances, but often he was made to work very hard by his new team-mate, a Formula One rookie by the name of Jacques Villeneuve. It made for a fascinating inter-team battle, two second-generation Formula One drivers fighting not only each other but the memory of their late and legendary fathers, Graham Hill and Gilles Villeneuve.

Villeneuve Jr had already created a sensation in the United States, where he had won the Indycar championship and the Indy 500. He made a startling Formula One debut in the Australian Grand Prix, bagging pole position and looking set to win until a late slide across the grass damaged a radiator and handed victory to Hill. Damon's greater experience showed over the season with a more consistent level of competitiveness, and he clinched the Championship in Japan with a mature drive to victory. Villeneuve, though, created some moments of spine-

▲ Jacques Villeneuve and Damon Hill at the British Grand Prix, Silverstone, in 1996.

tingling drama, never more so than at Estoril's final corner, when he did the unthinkable by overtaking Michael Schumacher round the outside.

Villeneuve vs Schumacher

Controversially, Williams didn't renew Damon Hill's contract for 1997, and he was replaced by Heinz-Harald Frentzen. This left Villeneuve to battle

with Schumacher's Ferrari for the world title. Their fortunes see-sawed through the season, and the showdown came in the final at Jerez, Spain. There, Schumacher was leading but Villeneuve, on new tyres, was catching fast after his pit stop. Electing to surprise the Ferrari driver, he made a move down the inside from a long way back. By the time Schumacher realized what was happening, it was too late. He turned in on the Williams, but succeeded only in bouncing off it and landing beached in the gravel trap. It left Villeneuve free to cruise to the title, though there was controversy in that he allowed the McLarens of Mika Häkkinen and David Coulthard to pass him in the late stages in exchange for their help earlier in the race, when they did not attack him in the midst of his battle with the Ferrari.

Ironically, one of the chief architects of this Williams World Championship, chief aerodynamicist Adrian Newey, had already left the team and headed for McLaren. This coincided with Renault withdrawing from official participation in the sport, leaving the Williams team's strength much reduced for the future. It would be some time before it recovered from such a double blow.

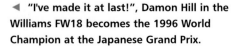

◄ "I've made it at last!", Damon Hill in the Williams FW18 becomes the 1996 World Champion at the Japanese Grand Prix.

▲ Hill with the 1996 World Championship trophy after winning the Japanese Grand Prix at Suzuka, 1996.

▲ Murray Walker (*left*), in his final Formula One race commentary for the BBC, interviews Hill, the new 1996 World Champion.

▼ Michael Schumacher turns his Ferrari into the passing Williams of Jacques Villeneuve, in a vain attempt to take his rival out of the race.

The McLaren Wonder Years

E verything conspired in McLaren's favour for the 1998 season. Formula One's technical regulations were radically altered just as brilliant aerodynamicist Adrian Newey arrived at the team. The Mercedes engines powering the cars were at the peak of their development, and the Bridgestone tyres gave them a performance advantage over the Goodyears on Michael Schumacher's Ferrari.

McLaren Overcome Restrictions

The FIA had been concerned about rising lap speeds, and their solution for 1998 was two-fold. Firstly, the maximum width of the cars was reduced from 2 metres to 1.8, so reducing the available ground effect-generating under-floor area, as well as limiting the mechanical grip. Secondly, slick tyres were outlawed and replaced by grooved tyres, giving a smaller surface area of rubber on the track. The effect was to make the cars more

▲ McLaren designer Adrian Newey.

▼ The McLarens of Häkkinen and Coulthard lead at the first corner of the Australian Grand Prix, Melbourne, in 1999.

skittery, and initially they were as much as 2 seconds per lap slower than they had been in 1997, though further technical development soon began to reduce this deficit.

The Cool Finn

McLaren's MP4-13 model brilliantly resolved the issues arising from the new regulations, and gave Mika Häkkinen and David Coulthard a flurry of victories. Ferrari fought back though, and came on very strong in the second half of the season. Michael Schumacher went to the final round in Japan with a chance of the title, but a dominant drive from Häkkinen sealed it for the Finn and his team.

Mika had a rather easier time of it in 1999 when Schumacher broke a leg in a crash at Silverstone. However, the strength of Ferrari showed when their number two driver, Eddie Irvine, took the title battle all the way to the final round. But again Häkkinen sealed it.

▼ David Coulthard in the McLaren MP4–14 at the Monaco Grand Prix in 1999.

▲ Mika Häkkinen and the McLaren MP4-13 took third place at the French Grand Prix at Magny-Cours in 1998.

▼ Häkkinen took third at the Malaysian Grand Prix at Sepang in 1999, this time driving the McLaren MP4-14.

Technology 1998

McLaren MP4-13

The new narrow-track/grooved tyre regulations of 1998 gave designers the chance to fundamentally re-evaluate the requirements rather than fine-honing existing themes. The McLaren design team, led by Adrian Newey, did this better than anyone else.

The tyre grooves substantially reduced the amount of rubber in contact with the track surface, placing mechanical grip at much more of a premium than before. Previously, aerodynamic performance had over-ruled all else, but McLaren actually surrendered some of that in order to claw back mechanical grip lost to the new regulations. In partnership with tyre suppliers Bridgestone, they opted for bigger front tyres, which more than made up in terms of grip what had been lost through increased drag. They gave the car a lower nose section too, reasoning that the limitation of under-body airflow would be more than compensated by the lowering of the centre of gravity.

Powered by a Mercedes-Benz V10 engine that produced 800bhp, it was the fastest car, and gave the McLaren team its first world title for seven years.

▼ Häkkinen's McLaren MP4-13 at the Hungarian Grand Prix in 1998.

The 21-year Itch

Michael Schumacher's dream of bringing world championship glory back to Ferrari finally came true in 2000, five years after joining. In each of those years the team were successively more competitive, as designer Rory Byrne and technical director Ross Brawn fine-honed their use of the huge resources at their disposal. The Ferrari F1-2000 was the first car to be created from the on-site wind tunnel. A 90-degree vee angle in its V10 lowered the centre of gravity from the previous motor's 80-degree angle. New materials enabled the cylinder heads to be smaller and lighter.

For each of the previous three years, Ferrari had to develop their way to mid-season competitiveness after beginning the season trailing either Williams or McLaren on speed. This car was fast right from the off – and that made the critical difference. Schumacher won the first three Grands Prix of the year and over the course of the season took a

▲ Ferrari's Michael Schumacher is elated after winning at Japan in 2000, while Mika Häkkinen (*far left*) and David Coulthard (*right*), for McLaren, look somewhat less so.

▼ The start of the Japanese Grand Prix, 2000. Häkkinen gets the jump on Schumacher.

further six. He clinched the title by winning an incredibly tense duel in Japan against his only rival, McLaren's Mika Häkkinen.

This was the first time since Jody Scheckter's 1979 success that a Ferrari driver had won the world title. The

▼ Luca di Montezemolo (*right*), president of Ferrari, talks with Hiroshi of Bridgestone tyres at the San Marino Grand Prix, 2002.

team president Luca di Montezemolo was present in Japan to witness the culmination of the work he had begun when he took up the post nine years earlier, when the team had been in

complete disarray. His dream had converged with that of Schumacher, Brawn and Byrne, the three men who had already won world titles together at Benetton.

▲ Michael Schumacher, in the Ferrari F1-2000, leads team-mate Rubens Barrichello at the British Grand Prix, Silverstone, in 2000. Schumacher took third place in the race.

Shapers

Ross Brawn

Brawn became best-known as the man whose brilliant pit strategies at both Benetton and Ferrari won countless races for Michael Schumacher. But as technical director of Ferrari, he was also an organizational genius with the necessary technical background to structure the Italian team in a way that brought the longest period of sustained success in its long history.

Brawn had been a highly successful designer before his partnership with Rory Byrne enabled him to step back. He began his motor racing career in 1976 as a research and development engineer at Williams. There, he learned an enormous amount from resident design chief Patrick Head in all aspects of Formula One car design. After spells as chief designer at Beatrice and

Arrows, he was recruited by Tom Walkinshaw's TWR team and designed the fabulously successful Jaguar XJR-14 sports racer. When Walkinshaw bought into the Benetton Formula One team, Brawn went with him, and worked alongside Rory Byrne for the first time. Here, the golden partnership took form. When Michael Schumacher joined the team, the triangle was complete.

For only one year – 1996, when Schumacher joined Ferrari but Brawn and Byrne stayed at Benetton – was the partnership broken up. Never have three such brilliant individuals worked together for so long in Formula One. That in itself goes a long way to explaining their success.

◄ Ferrari technical director Ross Brawn.

Ferrari Break All Records

Ferrari and Michael Schumacher actually strengthened their hold on Formula One during 2001 and 2002. The German superstar gave the Italian marque the greatest run of sustained success in its long and glorious history, and in the process he made himself the most statistically successful Formula One driver of all time.

In the 2001 Hungarian Grand Prix he clinched his fourth world title and equalled the record of 51 Grand Prix victories secured by Alain Prost eight years earlier. At the very next race, at Spa in Belgium, Schumacher surpassed that record. By the end of 2002 he had secured his fifth World Drivers' Championship, equalling the all-time record of Juan Manuel Fangio, and his career race win tally stood at an astonishing 64. Ferrari also took its fourth consecutive World Constructors' Championship in this year, a feat it had never before achieved. In winning 11 Grands Prix in 2002 alone, Schumacher also set the benchmark for the number of victories during a season, beating a record he had previously shared with Nigel Mansell.

◀ Ferrari's Michael Schumacher makes his trademark victory leap on the podium after winning the Spanish Grand Prix in 2002. McLaren's David Coulthard (*right*) finished in third place.

▼ (*left*) Rubens Barrichello's Ferrari F2002 (*below*) inches past team-mate Michael Schumacher to take an unexpected victory at the United States Grand Prix, Indianapolis, 2002.

Behind the awesome numbers lay Ferrari's ever-greater technical resource, and the brilliant use made of it by Rory Byrne and his design team. But in 2001 the Ferrari, while the fastest all-round car, was frequently out-powered by the BMW motor in the Williams chassis. When Formula One rookie Juan Pablo Montoya aggressively took his Williams past Schumacher's Ferrari to lead the Brazilian Grand Prix, many heralded the arrival of a new challenge to Schumacher's dominance. But despite several more exciting dices with the champion, Montoya's competitive circumstances actually declined in 2002 as the Williams FW24 proved no match for the F2002 Ferrari.

At the 2002 Italian Grand Prix, BMW proudly announced that its engine was the first in Formula One to break the 19,000rpm barrier. At this astronomical speed, the 3-litre V10 motor was achieving around 880 horsepower, making it the most powerful engine in Formula One.

BMW had re-entered Formula One with Williams in 2000. Also returning at that time was French tyre company Michelin, absent since 1984 and looking to break Bridgestone's dominance. With Williams in 2001 and 2002, and McLaren in 2002, Michelin returned to the race winner's circle, but the dominance of the Bridgestone-shod Ferrari meant such victories were perhaps fewer than their product warranted, a situation Michelin shared with BMW.

It was an illustration of how the various facets of the sport were being dwarfed by the scale of Ferrari's dominance – to the extent that calls were being made to liven up what was becoming an overly predictable show. Ferrari had courted controversy in Austria in 2002 when it instructed its second driver, Rubens Barrichello, who had led all the way, to move over in the last few hundred yards and hand victory to Schumacher. After the championship was sewn up several other races were stage-managed between the Ferrari drivers, such was their dominance. It was a development that did not go down well with fans of the sport.

Among moves being considered by the governing body were weight penalties for success and a new system of driver contracts that could see them change team for each race. That such radical departures were being contemplated illustrated the staggering extent of Ferrari's superiority.

▲ Juan Pablo Montoya in the Williams-BMW FW24 *(left)* and team-mate Ralf Schumacher, *(right)* squeeze out Schumacher's Ferrari F2002.

▼ Michael Schumacher *(left)* collects his Drivers' Championship Trophy at the FIA Prize Gala, while Jean Todt *(centre)* collects the Constructors' Trophy for Ferrari.

Schumacher Knocks 'em for Six

Ferrari's Michael Schumacher broke the all-time World Championship record in 2003 by scoring his sixth title. The previous record – Juan Manuel Fangio's five – had stood for 46 years. However, in contrast to the one-way dominance of Ferrari in 2002, the 2003 season was a classic, with a superbly tight battle for the World Championship between four drivers from three different teams.

Schumacher's 2002 dominance had led to falling television viewing figures. The governing body's response was a new set of sporting regulations for 2003. The points scoring system was revised, with a smaller gap between first and second and points down to eighth place instead of sixth – all designed to keep the title fight running longer. One-lap qualifying, whereby each driver took to the track on his own and had only one chance in which to set a time that would determine his grid position, was introduced. Furthermore, fuel could not be added to the car between qualifying and the race – meaning that there was a trade-off to be made between qualifying speed and pit stop strategies. These latter two changes had the effect of mixing the grids up slightly. But the

biggest contribution to the closely-matched 2003 competition was the improvement in the speed of the Williams-BMW and McLaren-Mercedes teams, aided considerably in both cases by the big advances made by their tyre supplier, Michelin. The rival Bridgestone

▲ **Juan Pablo Montoya's win at Monaco kick-started the Williams team's 2003 season.**

◄ **McLaren's Kimi Raikkonen took his first Formula One victory in the 2003 Malaysian Grand Prix, and pushed Michael Schumacher for the world title throughout the season.**

tyres, so dominant the year before, were left trailing, and this left Ferrari facing up to a very tough job.

Ferrari used its 2002 title-winning car for the first four races of the new season, while its new F2003-GA model underwent further development. Michael Schumacher won only one of those four races, and it became clear that he had a bigger fight on his hands than in the previous year. He gave the old car a glorious send-off by winning the San Marino Grand Prix. Two weeks later the new model, with a longer wheelbase, enhanced aerodynamics and more powerful engine, was given a victorious debut by Schumacher in the Spanish Grand Prix. Further wins in Austria and Canada meant that at the season's halfway point he appeared to be on-course to correct his shaky start to the year.

As it transpired, that Canadian win would be his last for quite some time. The Williams team had raced its new FW25 model from the beginning of the year. Radically different to its 2002 predecessor, with a much shorter wheelbase and Ferrari-like compact gearbox, it took the team some time to fully understand how to extract its full potential in terms of mechanical and aerodynamic set-up. The breakthrough came at the Monaco Grand Prix where Juan Pablo Montoya took an impressive victory. From this point onwards, the Williams was usually the fastest car around. In fact, the biggest problem for the team was that its two drivers, Montoya and Ralf Schumacher, were so closely matched that they were taking points off each other, as well as rival drivers from other teams.

Meanwhile, McLaren's Kimi Raikkonen kept scoring high places, adding to his victory in Malaysia, the second round of the series. McLaren had modified their 2002 car, with which to start the season, and the initial plan had been to then replace it with the radical new MP4-18. Development hitches with that car, and the continuing success of the MP4-17D, meant that the new car never did appear. Raikkonen's strong finishing record kept him in contention for the title right until the final round.

Raikkonen's team-mate David Coulthard won the opening round, in Australia, but otherwise had a rather low-key season. Michael Schumacher's team-mate at Ferrari, Rubens Barrichello, won the British Grand Prix in a superlative display and sealed Schumacher's title by winning in the final round, in Japan. In the two races prior to this, Schumacher had returned to winning form.

Giancarlo Fisichella gave the Jordan team a freak victory in an accident-shortened and very wet Brazilian Grand Prix. The season's other winner was Spanish newcomer, Fernando Alonso, driving for the Renault team. Aged just 22 years and 26 days, Alonso became the youngest ever Grand Prix winner, and the first from Spain, when he took victory in the Hungarian Grand Prix. Having withdrawn as an engine supplier after winning the 1997 World Championship with Williams, Renault had returned as a fully-fledged team in 2000 when it bought out Benetton. Under the control of former Benetton boss Flavio Briatore, Renault became increasingly competitive, and Alonso's result in Hungary marked its first victory as a team, rather than an engine supplier, for 20 years.

▲ Michael Schumacher was made to work hard for his win in the 2003 Spanish Grand Prix by Fernando Alonso's Renault.

► Schumacher celebrates his record-breaking sixth world title.

Statistics

World Champion Drivers

1950 Giuseppe Farina (Italy)
1951 Juan Manuel Fangio (Argentina)
1952 Alberto Ascari (Italy)
1953 Alberto Ascari (Italy)
1954 Juan Manuel Fangio (Argentina)
1955 Juan Manuel Fangio (Argentina)
1956 Juan Manuel Fangio (Argentina)
1957 Juan Manuel Fangio (Argentina)
1958 Mike Hawthorn (Britain)
1959 Jack Brabham (Australia)
1960 Jack Brabham (Australia)
1961 Phil Hill (USA)
1962 Graham Hill (Britain)
1963 Jim Clark (Britain)
1964 John Surtees (Britain)
1965 Jim Clark (Britain)
1966 Jack Brabham (Australia)
1967 Denny Hulme (New Zealand)
1968 Graham Hill (Britain)
1969 Jackie Stewart (Britain)
1970 Jochen Rindt (Austria)
1971 Jackie Stewart (Britain)
1972 Emerson Fittipaldi (Brazil)
1973 Jackie Stewart (Britain)
1974 Emerson Fittipaldi (Brazil)
1975 Niki Lauda (Austria)
1976 James Hunt (Britain)
1977 Niki Lauda (Austria)
1978 Mario Andretti (USA)
1979 Jody Scheckter (South Africa)
1980 Alan Jones (Australia)
1981 Nelson Piquet (Brazil)
1982 Keke Rosberg (Finland)
1983 Nelson Piquet (Brazil)
1984 Niki Lauda (Austria)
1985 Alain Prost (France)
1986 Alain Prost (France)
1987 Nelson Piquet (Brazil)
1988 Ayrton Senna (Brazil)
1989 Alain Prost (France)
1990 Ayrton Senna (Brazil)
1991 Ayrton Senna (Brazil)
1992 Nigel Mansell (Britain)
1993 Alain Prost (France)
1994 Michael Schumacher (Germany)
1995 Michael Schumacher (Germany)
1996 Damon Hill (Britain)
1997 Jacques Villeneuve (Canada)
1998 Mika Häkkinen (Finland)
1999 Mika Häkkinen (Finland)
2000 Michael Schumacher (Germany)
2001 Michael Schumacher (Germany)
2002 Michael Schumacher (Germany)
2003 Michael Schumacher (Germany)

World Champion Constructors

1958 Vanwall
1959 Cooper
1960 Cooper
1961 Ferrari
1962 BRM
1963 Lotus
1964 Ferrari
1965 Lotus
1966 Brabham
1967 Brabham
1968 Lotus
1969 Matra
1970 Lotus
1971 Tyrrell
1972 Lotus
1973 Lotus
1974 McLaren
1975 Ferrari
1976 Ferrari
1977 Ferrari
1978 Lotus
1979 Ferrari
1980 Williams
1981 Williams
1982 Ferrari
1983 Ferrari
1984 McLaren
1985 McLaren
1986 Williams
1987 Williams
1988 McLaren
1989 McLaren
1990 McLaren
1991 McLaren
1992 Williams
1993 Williams
1994 Williams
1995 Benetton
1996 Williams
1997 Williams
1998 McLaren
1999 Ferrari
2000 Ferrari
2001 Ferrari
2002 Ferrari
2003 Ferrari

Grands Prix Formulae

1906	Max weight 1000kg
1907	Max weight 1000kg
	Fuel consumption: 30 litres/100km (9.4mpg)
1908	Max weight 1150kg
	Max cylinder bore: 4-cylinder engines: 155mm
	6-cylinder engines: 127mm
1912	Max width 175cm
1913	Min weight 800kg
	Max weight 1100kg
	Fuel consumption: 20 litres/100km (14.1mpg)
1914	4.5-litre max
	Max weight 1100kg
1921	3-litre max
	Min weight 800kg
1922–25	2-litre max
	Min weight 650kg
1926–27	1.5-litre max
(1926)	Min weight 600kg
(1927)	Min weight 700kg
1928	Min weight 500kg
	Max weight 750kg
1929–30	Min weight 900kg
	Fuel consumption: 14 litres/100km (20.1mpg)
1931–33	No stipulation
1934–37	Max weight 750kg
1938–39	3-litre forced induction
	4.5-litre normally aspirated
1947–51	1.5-litre forced induction
	4.5-litre normally aspirated
1952–53	2-litre normally aspirated
	0.5-litre forced induction
1954–60	2.5-litre normally aspirated
	0.75-litre forced induction
1961–65	1.5-litre norm.aspirated only
	Min weight 450kg
1966–85	3-litre normally-aspirated
	1.5-litre forced induction
(1966–68)	Min weight 500kg
(1969–81)	Min weight 530kg
(1982)	Min weight 580kg
(1983)	Min weight 540kg
	Forced induction fuel max 250 litres
(1984–85)	Min weight 540kg
	Forced induction fuel max 220 litres. No fuel stops
1986	1.5-litre forced induction
	Min weight 540kg. Fuel max 195 litres. No fuel stops
1987	1.5-litre forced induction
	3.5-litre normally aspirated
	Forced induction fuel max 195 litres. Forced induction boost 4-bar max. No fuel stops. Min weight 540kg
1988	1.5-litre forced induction
	3.5-litre normally aspirated
	Forced induction fuel max 150 litres. Forced induction boost 2.5-bar max. No fuel stops. Forced induction 540kg. Normally aspirated 500kg
1989–94	3.5-litre normally-aspirated only. Min weight 500kg
(1994)	Fuel stops allowed
1995–present	3-litre normally aspirated only. Fuel stops allowed. Min weight 600kg including driver
(1999–present)	10-cylinder engines only

Engine Championship Race Wins

Ford Cosworth DFV	155	(1967–83)
Renault V10	75	(1989–97)
Ferrari Martinelli V10	47	(1996–03)
Honda turbo V6	40	(1984–88)
Ferrari Forghieri flat-12	37	(1970–79)
Mercedes Ilmor V10	32	(1997–03)
Porsche TAG turbo V6	25	(1984–87)
Coventry Climax V8	23	(1961–65)
Renault turbo V6	20	(1979–86)
Ford Cosworth HB	19	(1989–94)
Coventry Climax 4	17	(1958–61)
Ferrari Lampredi straight-4	16	(1952–55)
Honda Goto V10	16	(1989–90)
Ferrari Forghieri turbo V6	15	(1981–88)
Honda Goto V12	13	(1991–92)

Alfa Romeo straight-8	12	(1950–51)
BRM V8	12	(1962–66)
Ferrari Lombardi V12	11	(1989–95)
Maserati straight-6	9	(1953–57)
BMW turbo 4	9	(1982–86)
BMW V10	9	(2001–03)
Mercedes straight-8	9	(1954–55)
Vanwall straight-4	9	(1957–58)
Repco V8	8	(1966–67)
Ferrari Chiti V6	6	(1961–63)
Ferrari Jano V6	5	(1958–60)
Lancia V8	5	(1956)
BRM V12	4	(1970–72)
Mugen Honda V10	4	(1996–99)
Ferrari Lampredi V12	3	(1951)
Ferrari Bellai V8	3	(1964)
Ferrari Colombo V12	3	(1966–68)
Matra V12	3	(1977–81)
Ford Cosworth CR V10	2	(1995–03)
Maserati V12	2	(1966–67)
BRM straight 4	1	(1959)
BRM H16	1	(1966)
Honda Nakamura V12	1	(1965)
Honda Irimagiri V12	1	(1967)
Porsche flat-8	1	(1962)
Weslake V12	1	(1967)
Renault 111-deg V10	1	(2003)

Engine Championship Race Wins by Manufacturer

Ford	176
Ferrari	161
Renault	96
Honda	75
Mercedes	42
Coventry Climax	40
Porsche	26
BMW	18
BRM	18
Alfa Romeo	12
Maserati	11
Vanwall	9
Repco	8
Lancia	5
Matra	3
Weslake	1

Top 10 Youngest Championship Grand Prix Winners

Fernando Alonso
 22 years, 26 days (2003)
Bruce McLaren
 22 years, 80 days (1958)
Jacky Ickx
 22 years, 104 days (1968)
Michael Schumacher
 23 years, 188 days (1992)
Emerson Fittipaldi
 23 years, 296 days (1970)
Mike Hawthorn
 24 years, 86 days (1953)
Jody Scheckter
 24 years, 131 days (1974)
Elio de Angelis
 24 years, 148 days (1982)
David Coulthard
 24 years, 181 days (1995)
Peter Collins
 24 years, 208 days (1956)

Top 10 Oldest Championship Grand Prix Winners

Luigi Fagioli
 53 years, 22 days (1951)
Giuseppe Farina
 46 years, 276 days (1955)
Juan Manuel Fangio
 46 years, 41 days (1957)
Piero Taruffi
 45 years, 219 days (1952)
Jack Brabham
 43 years, 339 days (1970)
Nigel Mansell
 41 years, 97 days (1994)
Maurice Trintignant
 40 years, 200 days (1958)
Graham Hill
 40 years, 90 days (1969)
Clay Regazzoni
 39 years, 312 days (1979)
Carlos Reutemann
 39 years, 35 days (1981)

Top 10 Youngest Championship Grand Prix Participants

Mike Thackwell
 19 years, 82 days (1980)
Ricardo Rodriguez
 19 years, 209 days (1961)
Fernando Alonso
 19 years, 261 days (2001)
Esteban Tuero
 19 years, 320 days (1998)
Chris Amon
 19 years, 326 days (1963)
Jenson Button
 20 years, 52 days (2000)
Eddie Cheever
 20 years, 54 days (1978)
Tarso Marques
 20 years, 71 days (1996)
Peter Collins
 20 years, 94 days (1952)
Rubens Barrichello
 20 years, 295 days (1993)

World Championship Points Systems

1950–59:	8-6-4-3-2 for first five places in race. 1 point for fastest lap.
1959–90:	9-6-4-3-2-1 for first six places.
1991–2002:	10-6-4-3-2-1 for first six places.
2003–on:	10-8-6-5-4-3-2-1 for first eight places.

(shortened races awarded half-points)

Closest Grand Prix finishes

Italy 1971	0.010 secs	(Peter Gethin/ Ronnie Peterson)
USA 2002	0.011 secs	(Rubens Barrichello/ Michael Schumacher)
Spain 1986	0.050 secs	(Ayrton Senna/ Nigel Mansell)
Austria 1982	0.080 secs	(Elio de Angelis/ Keke Rosberg)
France 1954	0.100 secs	(Juan Manuel Fangio/ Karl Kling)
France 1961	0.100 secs	(Giancarlo Baghetti/ Dan Gurney)
Austria 2002	0.182 secs	(Michael Schumacher/ Rubens Barrichello)
Britain 1955	0.200 secs	(Stirling Moss/ Juan Manuel Fangio)
Holland 1955	0.200 secs	(Juan Manuel Fangio/ Stirling Moss)
Italy 1967	0.200 secs	(John Surtees/ Jack Brabham)
Spain 1981	0.210 secs	(Gilles Villeneuve/ Jacques Laffite)
Monaco 1992	0.215 secs	(Ayrton Senna/ Nigel Mansell)
Holland 1985	0.232 secs	(Niki Lauda/Alain Prost)
Hungary 1990	0.288 secs	(Thierry Boutsen/ Ayrton Senna)
Switzerland 1950	0.300 secs	(Giuseppe Farina/ Luigi Fagioli)
France 1956	0.300 secs	(Peter Collins/ Eugenio Castellotti)
Austria 1999	0.313 secs	(Eddie Irvine/ David Coulthard)
Holland 1978	0.320 secs	(Mario Andretti/ Ronnie Peterson)
France 1993	0.342 secs	(Alain Prost/ Damon Hill)
Japan 1991	0.344 secs	(Gerhard Berger/Ayrton Senna)

Index

PICTURE CREDITS
All photographs supplied by
Sutton Motorsport Images
except for the following.
t = top; b = bottom; l = left;
r = right; c = centre
Ludvigsen Library 24bl, br; 25t, b.
National Motor Museum 17t; 22t; 23b;
26b; 29tl, b; 30b; 31t.